JAN VENOLIA

WRITE RIGHT!

THIRD EDITION

A Desktop Digest of Punctuation, Grammar, and Style

TEN SPEED PRESS

PERIWINKLE PRESS

Also written by Jan Venolia

Better Letters: A Handbook of Business and Personal Correspondence

Rewrite Right! How to Revise Your Way to Better Writing

1◉

Ten Speed Press
P.O. Box 7123
Berkeley, California 94707

Cover Design by Fifth Street Design
Book Design by Nancy Austin
Illustrations by Ellen J. Sasaki

Library of Congress Cataloging-in-Publication Data

Write Right! : a desktop digest of punctuation, grammar, and style
/ Jan Venolia.

     p.   cm.

Includes bibliographical references (p.   ) and index.

ISBN 0-89815-676-9 (paper) : ISBN 0-89815-692-0 (spiral)

1. English language—Grammar.   2. English language—Punctuation.
3. English language—Style.   I. Title

PE1112.V4

428.2—dc20   95-1588

                             CIP

Printed in the United States of America

10 9 8 7 6 5 4 3 2 1 - 99 98 97 96 95

Despite the modern desire to be easy and casual, Americans from time to time give thought to the language they use.

—Wilson Follett

This book is for those times.

Abandon hopefully, all ye who enter here ☆

☆ SIGN ABOVE EDWIN NEWMAN'S DOOR

See Confused and Abused Words, p. 103

Contents

Who, Me? Learn to Write Better?   1

Punctuation Pointers   5

Mechanics   43

Grammatical Guidelines   69

Style   89

Confused & Abused Words   103

Appendix   125
  Venolia's Reverse Rules for Writers   126
  Glossary   128
  Bibliography   140
  Grammar Hotlines   142
  Frequently Misspelled Words   143
  Index   149

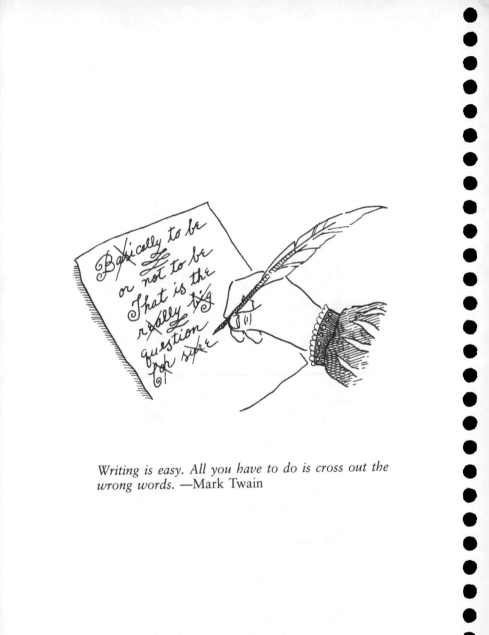

Writing is easy. All you have to do is cross out the wrong words. —Mark Twain

Who, Me? Learn to Write Better?

Yes, you. All of us need help with writing, at least occasionally. We have the impression that when school days are over, independent clauses and dangling modifiers become irrelevant. Belatedly, we discover that good writing is fundamental to good business.

The original edition of *Write Right!* was written for just such circumstances—to help readers catch their most common mistakes. I had noticed that people tend to repeat the same kinds of errors, and that correcting those errors markedly improves writing. It's now fifteen years later, and time to reevaluate *Write Right!* for its pertinence to our speeded-up, interactive world.

Electronic innovations have changed the way we conduct business and given us new tools. Word processors were rare when *Write Right!* first appeared, but today they are almost as common as TV sets in the home; computers have become indispensable in business, and communication via modem and fax is standard practice.

Individuals who used to rely on secretaries for correct spelling and grammar now do their own "keyboarding." Under pressures of time, they cut corners, producing sloppy writing that resembles speech. Does that matter? Are punctuation and spelling as outmoded as a typewriter eraser? In the world of virtual reality and multimedia imagery, is there any place for the written word, let alone the well-written word?

In fact, good writing is as important as ever. What appears on computer screens and emerges from fax machines is writing, not speech. Speech is less precise than writing. We can bolster speech with gestures and facial expressions, and when our words produce puzzled looks, we can back up and clarify. Writing has no such advantages. The words on screen or paper must do the job by themselves. If we are to keep from gradually slipping into complete gibberish, rules of good writing are still essential.

There may even be an inverse relationship: The greater the urgency to communicate, and to communicate quickly, the more important that time be taken to make writing clear and to the point. A poorly written document might be misunderstood, requiring clarification; worse yet, it might be tossed aside unread.

Grammar and punctuation help readers know when to pause, what is important, and which items belong together. Rules of style turn writing that is properly punctuated, grammatically correct—and boring—into writing that holds the reader's interest.

Can you rely on software to improve your writing? Though spellcheckers are a useful backup in the search for typos and misspelled words, you should be aware of their limitations. They will accept as correct a phrase with legitimate, though wrong, words, such as "Their on they're own." And I have yet to find a grammarchecker that wasn't more trouble than it was worth. A concise handbook such as *Write Right!* remains your best bet for quick answers to writing problems.

The objective of good writing—to convey thoughts clearly and engagingly—hasn't changed in recent years. Language is fluid, however, and rules that once appeared ironclad are subject to revision. On the whole, the rules I presented in the First Edition of *Write Right!* still apply, but for this Third Edition I have updated them, adding some and deleting others. Someone wanting to know the current acceptability of such matters as using split infinitives or ending a sentence with a preposition will find answers here. Of necessity, I expanded the section covering frequently confused words; alas, more and more words are being misused.

Write Right! answers questions as they arise. It is not a short course of rules to memorize, but a handy tool to keep next to your keyboard or tucked in a desk drawer. You may find it helpful to skim through the pages to see how the book is organized. The punctuation marks most likely to cause problems are treated alphabetically in "Punctuation Pointers." "Mechanics," as its name suggests, covers such aspects of writing as abbreviations, capitalization, italics, and spelling. "Grammatical Guidelines" delves into matters of subject-verb agreement, parallel construction, and correct handling of modifiers. "Style" recommends ways to trim and improve writing and to avoid bias in language. "Confused & Abused Words" untangles words like *convince* and *persuade*, *disburse* and *disperse*, and updates usage of such words as *hopefully* and *contact*.

Refer to the Glossary in the Appendix for definitions if you're unfamiliar with any grammatical terms. There you will also find a list of frequently misspelled words, a bibliography, information about Grammar Hotlines, and a tongue-in-cheek review of some rules of grammar.

As in previous versions of *Write Right!*, the rules are illustrated with quotations that were chosen to edify and amuse. Throughout, Ellen Sasaki's whimsical drawings keep us from taking ourselves, and our rules, too seriously.

The written word will be around for a long time to come. I hope you will find that *Write Right!* helps you do a good job when you need to "put it in writing."

A comma sets off introductory elements.
See Rule 11 (d), p. 21.

Punctuation Pointers

Apostrophe   6

Colon   12

Comma   14

Dash   25

Ellipsis   27

Hyphen   28

Parentheses   32

Quotation Marks   34

Semicolon   38

Slash   40

Punctuation Pointers

Punctuation marks are among the best tools for guiding your readers. Think of them as language traffic signals: Slow Down, Come This Way, Notice This, Detour. Properly used punctuation helps readers grasp your meaning; misleading punctuation (say, the absence of a comma) slows readers down.

If you find a sentence particularly hard to punctuate, consider re-writing it; the problem may be one of style rather than punctuation. The well-written sentence almost punctuates itself.

The following punctuation marks are listed alphabetically for ease of reference.

The Apostrophe

The apostrophe has moved to the head of my list of most frequently misused punctuation marks. Not only is it sometimes omitted where it is needed, but even more often the apostrophe pops up where it doesn't belong.

Wrong: Who's chicken is tastiest?
Right: Whose chicken is tastiest?

Wrong: Tomato's for Sale
Right: Tomatoes for Sale

Wrong: The patent is our's.
Right: The patent is ours.

Pause before using an apostrophe to consider whether it fills any of the following needs.

1 Use an apostrophe to show possession.

a) With all singular words and with plural words that do not end in s, add 's.

writer's cramp	employee's paycheck
the witness's testimony	the nurse's uniform
children's hour	women's issues

This rule also applies to proper nouns.

Charles's haberdasher   Groucho Marx's mustache

If this produces an awkward possessive, add only an apostrophe or rewrite to avoid the need for one.

Awkward: Dickens's novels
Better: Dickens' novels *or* the novels of Dickens

b) With plural words that end with s, add only an apostrophe.

writers' conference	employees' union
witnesses' testimony	the nurses' duties
the Davises' vacation	the Morrises' house

Psychiatry enables us to correct our faults by confessing our parents' shortcomings.
—Laurence J. Peter

Be sure you have the plural form of the word before you add the apostrophe: the Morrises' house, *not* the Morris' house or the Morris's house.

Note: NEVER use an apostrophe with possessive pronouns (*its, hers, his, theirs, yours, ours, whose*); by definition, these words are already possessive. <u>Above all, do not add an apostrophe to the possessive pronoun *its*.</u>

Wrong: The apostrophe seems to have a life of it's own.

Right: The apostrophe seems to have a life of its own.

Remember that *it's* is a contraction for *it is* or *it has*.

Right: It's easy to put the apostrophe in its place.

THE DOG WAGGED TAIL.

"ITS"

c) If two or more individuals possess a single item, add *'s* to the last name only.

Tom and Dick's boat (one boat)

d) If two or more individuals possess two or more items, add *'s* to each noun.

Tom's and Dick's boats (two boats)

e) Treat possessives of compound words as follows:

With *singular* compound words, add *'s* to the end of the last word.

son-in-law's car   notary public's seal
Master-of-Ceremony's   major domo's baton
  greeting

With *plural* compound words, show possession with a phrase beginning with *of*.

Wrong: the attorneys general's meeting
Right: the meeting of the attorneys general

(See Rule 63d regarding formation of plural compounds.)

f) Use ' or 's in established idiomatic phrases even though ownership is not involved:

two dollars' worth   a month's vacation
a stone's throw   today's jittery market
five years' experience (*or* five years of experience)

Sometimes a hyphenated form is better: a two-week vacation.

g) Avoid using 's in the following cases:

With titles:

Poor: *Catcher in the Rye*'s ending
Better: the ending of *Catcher in the Rye*

With abbreviations or acronyms:

Poor: IRS' (or (IRS's) policies
Better: IRS policies

Although the possessive *'s* is often correct with inanimate objects (state's rights, the law's effect), use an *of* phrase where the possessive would be awkward.

Poor: the Tower of London's interior
Better: the interior of the Tower of London

Poor: the table's foot
Better: the foot of the table

If a name or title is more descriptive than possessive (e.g., Actors Equity, *Publishers Weekly*), omit the apostrophe—but watch for pitfalls. When I saw the following headline, I wondered how the employees had been "done" in the first place.

Wrong: Stanford Employees Report Being Redone
Right: Stanford Employees' Report Being Redone

2 Use an apostrophe in contractions to indicate omission of letters or numbers.

> summer of '42, can't, he's, they're, you'd

> *I'm not denyin' the women are foolish:*
> *God Almighty made 'em to match the men.*
> —George Eliot

> *The dubious privilege of a freelance writer is he's*
> *given the freedom to starve anywhere.*
> —S. J. Perlman

> *You'd be surprised how much it costs to look*
> *this cheap.* —Dolly Parton

Contractions create a friendly, informal tone, but you should avoid them in formal writing.

Formal: We will phone you as soon as the shipment arrives.
Informal: We'll be in touch shortly.

If you are uncertain whether you're using a contraction correctly, mentally return it to its uncontracted form to see if the sentence makes sense.

>   You're welcome to stay here. (*you are* welcome...)

>   Your welcome is assured. (possessive pronoun *your*)

3 **Use an apostrophe to form certain plurals.**

a) in abbreviations that have periods

>   M.D.'s   Ph.D.'s

b) with letters when the addition of *s* alone would be confusing

>   p's and q's
>   The instructor handed out few A's.

c) in words used merely as words without regard to their meaning

>   Don't give me any *if*'s, *and*'s, or *but*'s.

The Colon

The colon is a mark of anticipation, as the following rules illustrate.

4 **Use a colon as an introduction before a list, summary, long quotation, or final clause that explains or amplifies what precedes the colon.** Capitalize the first letter following the colon only if it begins a complete statement, a quotation, or more than one sentence. (See Rule 45.)

> *Santa Claus had the right idea: Visit people once a year.* —Victor Borge

> *Poetry always was, and always should be, preeminently that: significant sound.* —D. G. Bridson

5 Use a colon following the words *as follows* or *the following.*

> The ingredients of a diplomat's life are as follows: protocol, alcohol, and Geritol.

The concept of "as follows" may be implicit.

> *In our country we have three unspeakably precious things: freedom of speech, freedom of conscience, and the prudence never to practice either.* —Mark Twain

6 Use a colon in the following cases:

a) formal salutations

> Dear Senator Todd:

(See Rule 11i for punctuation of informal salutations.)

b) ratios

> 2:1

c) to indicate dialogue

> Margaret Fuller: I accept the universe.

> Thomas Carlyle: Gad! She'd better!

d) to separate a title and subtitle

Better Letters: A Handbook of Business & Personal Correspondence

---

Note: Do not use a colon immediately after a verb.

Wrong: Prerequisites for the course are: two years of history, Sociology 101, and the ability to speak Spanish.

Right: Prerequisites for the course are two years of history, Sociology 101, and the ability to speak Spanish.

The Comma

When you have trouble getting the commas right, chances are you're trying to patch up a poorly structured sentence. —Claire Kehrwald Cook

Too many commas make writing choppy; too few create misunderstanding. The following rules chart a course between the extremes.

7 Use a comma to separate independent clauses that are joined by such coordinating conjunctions as *and, but, or, nor, for, yet,* and *so.* (An independent clause, also known as the main clause, makes a complete statement.)

I respect faith, but doubt is what gets you an education.
—Wilson Mizner

The optimist proclaims that we live in the best of all possible worlds, and the pessimist fears this is true.
—James Branch Cabell

The English are not a very spiritual people, so they invented cricket to give them some idea of eternity.
—George Bernard Shaw

Unless a comma is required to prevent misreading, you may omit it between short, closely related clauses.

Keep your face to the sunshine and you cannot see the shadow.
—Helen Keller

We are born princes and the civilizing process turns us into frogs.
—Eric Berne

If the clauses are long and contain commas, use a semicolon rather than a comma to separate them.

If a man begins with certainties, he shall end in doubts; but if he will be content to begin with doubts, he shall end in certainties.
—Francis Bacon

Use a comma between the dependent and main clauses only when the dependent clause precedes the main clause. (Dependent clauses are incomplete statements; they are underlined in the following examples.)

As scarce as truth is, the supply has always been in excess of demand.
—Josh Billings

If you keep your mind sufficiently open, people will throw a lot of rubbish in it. —William A. Orton

8 Use commas to separate three or more items in a series.

Tom, Dick, and Harry

Early to rise and early to bed,
Makes a man healthy, wealthy, and dead.
—Ogden Nash

Although many of us were taught that the final comma is optional, it is now considered mandatory. Using a comma before the last item in a series avoids possible confusion. The hazards of omitting the final comma are evident in the following example.

Clean sheets, the smell of freshly baked bread and my kid sister all remind me of home.

The elements in a series may be short independent clauses.

> *The only way to keep your health is to eat what you don't want, drink what you don't like, and do what you'd rather not.* —Mark Twain

> *Animals have these advantages over man: They have no theologians to instruct them, their funerals cost them nothing, and no one starts lawsuits over their wills.* —Voltaire

When the elements in the series are joined by conjunctions such as *and* or *or*, omit the commas.

> *As soon as questions of will or decision or reason or choice of action arise, human science is at a loss.* —Noam Chomsky

9 **Use commas between consecutive adjectives that modify the same noun.**

> an inexpensive, worthwhile program

(Both "inexpensive" and "worthwhile" modify the noun "program.")

> *Conscience is a still, small voice that makes minority reports.* —Franklin P. Jones

When the first adjective modifies not the noun alone but a combination of the second adjective and the noun, omit the comma.

> average urban voter   cold roast beef
> white tennis shoes   short time span

("Average" modifies "urban voter," not just "voter"; "white" modifies "tennis shoes," and so on.)

One way to determine whether consecutive adjectives modify the same noun (*a young, energetic student*) is to insert the word *and* between the adjectives. "Young and energetic student" makes sense, but "short and time span" doesn't. Use a comma only between adjectives where *and* would be a plausible alternative.

white tennis shoes   *ugly, old fur coat*

The phrase "an ugly, old fur coat" illustrates both where to use a comma and where to omit it. "Ugly and old" sounds right, but "old and fur coat" doesn't; hence, only *ugly* and *old* are separated by a comma.

10 Use commas where needed for clarity.

a) to separate identical or similar words

> Whatever you do, do it right.

b) to provide a pause or avoid confusion

> If he chooses, Williams can take over the program.

> Once you understand, the reason is clear.

Most of us would momentarily misread sentences such as the following, from which I removed the commas.

> There were no frontiers left behind which one could hide.

> *As the corpse went past the flies left the restaurant table in a cloud and rushed after it.*
> —George Orwell

c) to indicate omission of a word or words

> *When angry, count ten before you speak; if very angry, a hundred.* —Thomas Jefferson

11 Use a comma to set off certain elements.

a) contrasting words or phrases

> *Advice is judged by results, not by intentions.*
> —Cicero

> *The fool wonders, the wise man asks.*
> —Benjamin Disraeli

> *The less you write, the better it must be.*
> —Jules Renard

b) phrases that are parenthetical, disruptive, or out of order

Pessimism, when you get used to it, is just as agreeable as optimism. —Arnold Bennett

Great blunders are often made, like large ropes, of a multitude of fibers. —Victor Hugo

Every man is, or hopes to be, an idler.
—Samuel Johnson

c) nonrestrictive phrases

As their name suggests, nonrestrictive phrases add non-essential information. If the nonrestrictive phrase is in the middle of the sentence, be sure to enclose it in a *pair* of commas; this helps the reader bridge the gap between what precedes and what follows the phrase.

The greatest discovery of my generation is that human beings, by changing the inner attitudes of their minds, can change the outer aspects of their lives. —William James

To knock a thing down, especially if it is cocked at an arrogant angle, is a deep delight of the blood.
—George Santayana

An appositive (an explanatory equivalent that immediately follows the word it explains) is often a nonrestrictive phrase.

My mother, the family historian, obtained startling information from the Marriage License Bureau.

Omit the commas if the phrase is defining (restrictive). In the following examples, the restrictive phrases are underlined; they define *which* form of taxation, *which* conservative, and *which* radical.

Inflation is the one form of taxation <u>that can be imposed without legislation</u>. —Milton Friedman

The conservative <u>who resists change</u> is as valuable as the radical <u>who proposes it</u>. —Will and Ariel Durant

d) introductory phrases

On second thought, when the meek eventually inherit the earth it will probably be in such a condition that nobody would have it.
—Laurence J. Peter

Fortunately, there are those among us who have a healthy irreverence toward power, even as they seek it. —Weir Reed

In the long run, it is the sum total of the actions of millions of individuals that constitutes effective group action. —Paul Ehrlich

e) direct address

Reader, suppose you were an idiot. And suppose you are a member of Congress. But I repeat myself.
—Mark Twain

To lose one parent, Mr. Worthing, may be regarded as a misfortune; to lose both looks like carelessness.
—Oscar Wilde

I recently received a promotional letter with the following teaser on the envelope:

Are you always the first to know Jan Venolia?

Omission of a comma to set off my name (I was being addressed directly) changed the meaning in an unintended way.

f) direct quotation

> John Ciardi said, "A dollar saved is a quarter earned."

> *"Take some more tea," the March Hare said to Alice, very earnestly. "I've had nothing yet," Alice replied in an offended tone, "so I can't take more." "You mean you can't take less," said the Hatter. "It's very easy to take more than nothing."*
> —Lewis Carroll

(See Rule 31 regarding other punctuation of quotations.)

g) the words *for example,* *that is,* and *namely*

> The evidence all pointed to one conclusion; namely, the defendant was not guilty.

The abbreviations for these words are based on Latin words and should also be followed by commas.

> *for example = exempli gratia = e.g.*

> *that is = id est = i.e.*

> *namely = videlicet = viz.*

> She plans to introduce a proposal to streamline election procedures (i.e., to allow voting by mail).

h) conjunctive adverbs

Put a comma after adverbs that are functioning as conjunctions if you wish to indicate a pause. Examples of conjunctive adverbs are *however, therefore, indeed, thus,* and *consequently.*

> A shortage of platinum has halted production; consequently, we are unable to fill your order at this time.

Note that the adverb is preceded by a semicolon, not a comma. (See Rule 36.)

i) informal salutations

> Dear Tom,

j) dates

Put commas both before and after the year when a date is written in month-day-year order.

> Your letter of July 4, 1776, answers all my questions.

If the date is written in day-month-order, omit the commas.

> Your letter of 4 July 1776 answers all my questions.

12   Do *not* use commas in the following cases.

a) between independent clauses unless they are joined by *and, but, or, for, nor, yet,* or *so*

Wrong: The Dow industrials hit a new high, the dollar continued to recover.

Right: The Dow industrials hit a new high, and the dollar continued to recover.

Wrong: The proposal needs rewriting, however, it is a good start.

Right: The proposal needs rewriting; however, it is a good start.

Joining two independent clauses without a conjunction is called a *comma fault.* As with most rules, this one can occasionally be bent for effect.

> *We didn't lose any games last season, we just ran out of time twice.* —Vince Lombardi

b) between subject and verb

This error frequently occurs when a comma is placed *following* the last item in a series,

Wrong: Riding motorcycles, hang-gliding, and skydiving,
were the main pastimes in her short life.

or when the subject is a phrase.

Wrong: Placing a comma between subject and verb, is
incorrect.

c) between modifier and the word modified, unless what intervenes is parenthetical or nonrestrictive (See Rule 11c)

Wrong: a concise, readable, report
Right: a concise, readable report
Right: a concise, though readable, report

d) between elements of a compound predicate

Wrong: On Friday I phoned his office, and was told he
was not in.
Right: On Friday I phoned his office and was told he was
not in.

> *He sows hurry and reaps indigestion.*
> —Robert Louis Stevenson

e) between an independent and a dependent clause when the independent clause comes first (See Rule 7)

> *You never realize how short a month is until
> you pay alimony.* —John Barrymore

> *Everything is funny as long as it is happening to
> someone else.* —Will Rogers

The Dash

Dashes are attention-getters that can be effective when used judiciously. They may also indicate sloppy writing. Can you substitute a comma, colon, or parenthesis? Reserve the dash for those instances when you want a sharper break in continuity than commas would provide or a more dramatic aside than you would achieve with parentheses.

13 **Use the dash for emphasis, to indicate an abrupt change, or with explanatory words or phrases.**

> *It may be that the race is not always to the swift, nor the battle to the strong—but that is the way to bet.* —Damon Runyon

> *Most of us hate to see a poor loser—or a rich winner.* —Harold Coffin

Use a single dash to summarize, much as you would use a colon.

> *Nature gave man two ends—one to sit on and one to think with. Ever since then, man's success or failure has been dependent on the one he used most.* —George R. Kirkpatrick

Use a pair of dashes to enclose parenthetical elements.

> *Though motherhood is the most important of all the professions—requiring more knowledge than any other department in human affairs—there was no attention given to preparation for this office.* —Elizabeth Cady Stanton

Years ago, all anyone needed to know about typing a dash was that it consisted of two hyphens, with no spaces before, after, or between them. Today, desktop publishing allows refinements of the dash that produce copy resembling typeset material. The following information will help those with desktop publishing capabilities take full advantage of their equipment.

The em dash is the standard dash. Use it in text where the dash appears in lieu of commas or parentheses.

> *Anybody can win—unless there happens to be a second entry.* —George Ade

> *The business of government is to keep government out of business—that is, unless business needs government aid.* —Will Rogers

> *Civilization—the victory of persuasion over force.* —Palmer Wright

Longer dashes, called 3-em dashes, are used as follows:

- in bibliographies for successive works by the same author
- to indicate the omission of letters from words (Ms. J____, I'll be d____).

The en dash is shorter than the standard dash and longer than a hyphen. It is used between inclusive numbers, such as 1920–1930 or pp. 45–6.

Note: A hazard for those whose word processors don't have a dash is that the two hyphens which are used to represent the dash may become separated at the end of the line; if this happens, reunite the hyphens by forcing the line ending at the first hyphen.

The Ellipsis

Ellipsis points (three equally spaced periods) indicate an omission from quoted material or a trailing off of dialogue or thought. For most purposes, the following rules regarding number and spacing of the dots are sufficient. See *The Chicago Manual of Style* or *A Manual for Writers* by Kate Turabian for more formal specifications.

14 Use an ellipsis to indicate an omission within a quotation.

a) To show omission of a few words from the middle of a sentence, use three dots:

> *The salary of the chief executive of a large corporation...is frequently a warm personal gesture by the individual to himself.* —J. K. Galbraith

b) To show omission of whole sentences, add a fourth dot to represent the period at the end of the last sentence before the omission:

> *The speaker may be forgiven if he becomes entangled in a hopeless sentence structure, but not so the writer. ...The speaker can use intonation, facial expression, and gesture to help where his language is lame, but written words lie quietly on the page.*
> —Theodore Bernstein

You may use other punctuation on either side of the ellipsis points if it helps clarify the meaning.

> *Virtually every important domestic change in the United States in recent years has been bottom up. From civil rights to the women's movement to*

tax revolt, ...the public has been the leader and
the leadership has been the follower.
—Daniel Yankelovich

The Hyphen

15 Use a hyphen with certain prefixes and suffixes.

a) to avoid doubling or tripling a letter

semi-independent	anti-incumbent
shell-like	part-time

b) if the root word begins with a capital letter

un-American	non-Euclidean
pre-Christmas	post-World War II

c) in general, with the prefixes *all-*, *self-*, *ex-*, and *vice-*

all-knowing	self-made
ex-husband	vice-president
self-regulating	all-purpose

d) to avoid awkward pronunciations or ambiguity

un-ionized	anti-abortion
co-worker	re-read

16 Use a hyphen after a series of words having a common base that is not repeated.

first-, second-, and third-quarter earnings
small- and middle-sized companies

17 Use a hyphen to form certain compound words.

Compound words unite two or more words, with or without a hyphen, to convey a single idea. Generally, you should write compound words as one word (handgun, airborne, turnkey, stockbroker); however, retain the hyphen in the following cases:

a) in compound nouns, where needed for clarity or as an aid in pronunciation

right-of-way   editor-in-chief
decision-maker   president-elect
sit-in   come-on

Since television, the well-read are being taken over by the well-watched. —Mortimer Adler

30 odd guests

Omitting a needed hyphen can create confusing, and sometimes unintentionally humorous, phrases. For example, *free public domain software* might look like domain software that is free to the public, whereas *free public-domain software* is readily understood. *Self storage units* would be a place to store the self; *30 odd guests* would be unnecessarily insulting to your friends.

Be sure to hyphenate *all* the words that are to be linked in this way:

10-year-old boy, *not* 10-year old boy.

b) **in compound adjectives (unit modifiers) when they precede the word they modify**

well-to-do individual   solid-state circuit
cost-of-living increase   matter-of-fact statement
well-designed unit   up-to-date methods

The authors adopted an I-can-laugh-at-it-now-but-it-was-no-laughing-matter-at-the-time attitude.
—Theodore Bernstein

I can't take a well-tanned person seriously.
—Cleveland Amory

If the words that make up a compound adjective *follow* the words they modify and appear in a normal word order, they are no longer compound adjectives, and no hyphens are used.

The unit is well designed.

Their accounting methods are up to date.

Idiomatic usage retains the hyphen in certain compounds regardless of the order in which they appear in the sentence.

Tax-exempt bonds can be purchased.

The bonds are tax-exempt.

> *Note:* If each of the adjectives could modify the noun without the other adjective, more than a single idea is involved (i.e., it is not a compound adjective), and a hyphen is not used.
>
> a happy, healthy child
> a new digital alarm clock

c) with improvised compounds

know-it-all   stick-in-the-mud
Johnny-come-lately   ne'er-do-well

He spoke with a certain what-is-it in his voice, and I could see that if not actually disgruntled, he was far from being gruntled. —P. G. Wodehouse

18 Use a hyphen in fractions and compound numbers from 21 to 99.

three-fourths   thirty-seven
one-third   forty-two

19 Use a hyphen to combine numeral-unit adjectives.

12-inch ruler   5-cent cigar
30-day month   100-year lifespan

20 Use a hyphen to combine an initial capital letter with a word.

T-shirt	X-rated
U-turn	V-neck

21 Use a hyphen to divide a word at the right-hand margin. (See Rules 67-69)

(See Rule 46b regarding capitalization of hyphenated words.)

Note: Do not hyphenate adverbs ending in -*ly* when they are combined with an adjective or participle.

Wrong: widely-held beliefs
highly-regarded individual

Right: widely held beliefs
highly regarded individual

Parentheses

Parentheses have the effect of an aside, as if you were trying to say the words under your breath. Avoid overusing them.

22 Use parentheses to set off explanatory or peripheral matter.

> *It is only in good writing that you will find how words are best used, what shades of meaning they can be made to carry, and by what devices (or lack*

of them) the reader is kept going smoothly or bogged down. —Jacques Barzun

If the parenthetical matter has a close logical relationship to the rest of the sentence, use commas instead.

It is probably safe to say that, over a long period of time, political morality has been as high as business morality. —Henry Steele Commager

23 **Punctuate sentences with parentheses as follows:**

a) **When the parenthetical matter is a complete statement, enclose associated punctuation within the parentheses.**

He detected a distinct coolness in the reaction of the audience. (Events later confirmed his suspicions.)

In a surprising reversion to my childhood, I grabbed the garbage can lid and slid down the snowy slope. (Remember doing that?)

b) **When a parenthetical item falls in the middle or at the end of a sentence, place the necessary punctuation *after* the closing parenthesis.**

There is only one problem (and he admits it): his chronic tardiness.

I phoned him when I arrived (as I had promised).

Do not put a comma, semicolon, or dash before an opening parenthesis.

Wrong: I phoned him when I arrived, (as I had promised) but he was not at home.

Right: I phoned him when I arrived (as I had promised), but he was not at home.

Quotation Marks

24 **Use quotation marks for a direct quotation.**

> Oscar Levant said of a politician, "He'll double-cross that bridge when he gets to it."

Do not use quotation marks for an indirect quotation (that is, a restatement of someone's words).

> According to Robert Frost, a jury is twelve persons chosen to decide who has the better lawyer.

When a quotation consists of several paragraphs, do one of the following:

- Place a quotation mark at the beginning of each paragraph and at the end of the final paragraph.
- Indent and single-space the text, omitting the quotation marks.

25 **Use quotation marks to enclose a word or phrase that is being defined.**

> The word "ventana" is Spanish for window.

> "Qualifying small businesses" means those with fewer than 250 employees.

> *The two most beautiful words in the English language are "Check enclosed."* —Dorothy Parker

26   Use quotation marks to enclose words or phrases following such terms as *entitled, the word(s), the term, marked, designated, classified, named, endorsed,* or *signed.*

> The check was endorsed "John Hancock."

> *I always wanted to write a book that ended with the word "mayonnaise."* —Richard Brautigan

> *A commentary on the times is that the word "honesty" is now preceded by "old-fashioned."*
> —Larry Wolters

27   Use quotation marks to indicate a misnomer or special meaning for a word.

> Some "antiques" would be more accurately described as junk.

> *You may be sure that when a man begins to call himself a "realist," he is preparing to do something he is secretly ashamed of doing.* —Sydney Harris

It is easy to overdo this usage, resulting in a cloying, affected style.

> *Note:* Do not use quotation marks following the words *known as, called, so-called,* etc. unless the expressions that follow are misnomers or slang.
>
> > *Most of our so-called reasoning consists in finding arguments for going on believing as we already do.* —James Harvey Robinson

28 Use quotation marks to enclose the titles of *parts* of whole publications:

- chapters or other divisions of a book,
- articles in periodicals,
- stories, essays, poems, and the like, in anthologies or similar collections.

Italicize or underline titles of *whole* works, such as books, periodicals, plays, movies, and reports (for example, *Harper's, The Wizard of Oz*).

29 Use quotation marks to enclose titles of the following:

- songs
- television and radio programs

30 Use single quotation marks to indicate a quote within a quote.

> Friedrich Nietzsche said, "He who has a 'why' to live can bear almost any 'how'."

> Kin Hubbard wrote, "When a fellow says, 'It ain't the money but the principle of the thing,' it's the money."

31 **Punctuate material associated with quotation marks as follows:**

Place comma and final period *inside* the quotation marks; place other punctuation marks *outside* the quotation marks unless they are part of the material being quoted.

She had the audacity to say "No"!

Mae West is supposed to have said, "No gold-digging for me. ...I take diamonds!"

When asked by an anthropologist what America was called before the white man came, a Native American said simply, "Ours." —Vine Deloria, Jr.

Do you watch "60 Minutes"?

On being told that President Coolidge had just died, Dorothy Parker asked, "How could they tell?"

The Semicolon

The semicolon provides a stronger break than a comma, a weaker break than a period. It is a useful punctuation mark that a careful writer employs to good effect.

It is almost always a greater pleasure to come across a semicolon than a period. ...You get a pleasant feeling of expectancy; there is more to come; read on; it will get clearer. —George F. Will

32 **Use a semicolon between closely related independent clauses when they are not joined by a conjunction.**

The believer is happy; the doubter is wise.
—Hungarian proverb

Few people think more than two or three times a year; I have made an international reputation for myself by thinking once or twice a week.
—George Bernard Shaw

33 **Use a semicolon to separate long or complicated items in a series.**

The lottery winners included an elderly gentleman who had never before bought a lottery ticket; a high school student hoping to use the winnings for college expenses; and a reporter who had bought her ticket while covering corruption in the lottery system.

34 Use a semicolon between independent clauses that are long or contain commas.

> *If a man runs after money, he's money-mad; if he keeps it, he's a capitalist; if he spends it, he's a playboy; if he doesn't get it, he's a ne'er-do-well; if he doesn't try to get it, he's a parasite; and if he accumulates it after a lifetime of hard work, people call him a fool who never got anything out of life.*
> —Vic Oliver

35 Use a semicolon between explanatory phrases that are introduced by such words as *for example, that is,* or *namely.*

> The students are preparing sophisticated entries for next week's Science Fair; for example, one electronics whiz is building a robot.

36 Use a semicolon between the independent clauses of a compound sentence when they are linked by the following adverbs: *however, thus, accordingly, indeed,* and *therefore.* Linking the clauses with a comma instead of a semicolon creates a *comma fault.* (See Rules 11h and 12a.)

PROJECTIONS WERE GLOOMY
HOWEVER, SALES SKYROCKETED.

Wrong: The father of the guest of honor will be late for the ceremony, however, he does plan to attend.

Right: The father of the guest of honor will be late for the ceremony; however, he does plan to attend.

The Slash

The slash is also known as the *virgule, diagonal*, or *slant*. Although it appears in informal writing more frequently now than when *Write Right!* was first published, it is seldom appropriate in formal writing.

37 **In informal writing, use the slash as a stand-in for a word.**

- for the word *to* (price/earnings ratio);
- for the word *per* (100 miles/hour);
- for the word *or* (and/or, his/her);
- for the word *and* (the July/August issue).

However, not all uses of the slash can be justified. *And/or* smacks of legalese and can often be replaced by either *and* or *or*. I find *he/she* difficult to read, and *s/he* even more so. Whenever possible, use more gracious alternatives for avoiding gender bias. (See Rule 85.)

Occasionally, the slash indicates that the writer didn't take the time to think clearly and just cobbled together a couple of words for the reader to sort out. If a slash represents sloppy writing, rewrite for clarity.

Poor: The actress met with me to promote her movie and to dispel/explain her tumultuous offscreen image.

Better: The actress met with me to promote her movie and to dispel some of the myths behind her offscreen image.

From a letter to the editor of *The New York Times*, Thursday, September 14, 1989:

> *The neutral pronoun "he (slash) she"*
>   *has come into its glory.*
> *In conversations, though, some say,*
>   *it tends to sound quite gory.*
>
> *The British, in their wisdom, call*
>   *the "/" an oblique stroke,*
> *Which offers a solution for*
>   *the language as it's spoke.*
>
> *To dodge offensive references*
>   *say "he (oblique stroke) she."*
> *So no one claims that you endorse*
>   *such gross misogyny.*
>
> *For surely here's a case in which*
>   *we each react uniquely.*
> *Faced with a choice, would you opt to*
>   *be slashed—or stroked obliquely?*
>
> Don Hauptman
> New York, Aug. 27, 1989

But whether you call it *oblique stroke* or *slash,* I still don't like *he/she*!

Forming plurals. See Rule 50(c), p. 59.

Mechanics

Abbreviations   44

Capitalization   48

Italics   53

Numbers—Figures or Words?   55

Spelling   57

Word Division   64

43

Mechanics

Abbreviations

Perhaps no aspect of written language is changing more rapidly than abbreviations. Electronic networking and E-mail have made speed of transmission a primary consideration. Since shorter documents cost less to send, the language of online users is often riddled with abbreviations and acronyms.

Such shortcuts can be effective, but a word of caution is appropriate. When creating abbreviations or acronyms, don't sacrifice clarity for brevity. A short, incomprehensible document may cost more in the long run than a longer one that is easy to understand.

38 **Create abbreviations and acronyms as follows:**

a) **When abbreviating, omit most vowels (other than initial ones) and select consonants that give the best sense of the word.**

> "Office" becomes "ofc"
> "Management" becomes "Mgmt"
> "Department" becomes "Dept"

b) **Form acronyms from the initial letters in a name or by combining initial letters with parts of a series of words.**

Thus, MADD is derived from Mothers Against Drunk Driving and *radar* from <u>ra</u>dio <u>d</u>etecting <u>a</u>nd <u>r</u>anging.

Occasionally initial letters of prepositions and articles are omitted or added in order to achieve a manageable or memorable acronym. The National Organization for Women chose to omit the preposition "for" when creating the acronym NOW, while the government plucked the "c" from the middle of the world "intercontinental" when creating the acronym ICBM (intercontinental ballistic missile), in order to avoid offending a large corporation.

c) Use *a* or *an* with an acronym according to the initial *sound*.

The choice of the article *a* or *an* preceding an acronym or abbreviation is determined by how we pronounce the word, not by whether it begins with a vowel or consonant. Certain consonants (F, H, L, M, N, R, S, and X) are pronounced as if they began with a vowel (*f* is pronounced "ef," *r* is pronounced "ahr," etc.). Thus, when we pronounce the individual letters in an abbreviation beginning with one of these consonants (an MBA degree), *an* is correct. However, if we say the acronym as a word (a MADD educational program), *a* is correct.

> a NASA program, *but* an NTSB ruling
> a LAN user, *but* an L.A. radio station

39 Abbreviate addresses as follows:

a) Use two capital letters and no period for the state abbreviation in an outside address (the address on the envelope). For example, write New York as NY (not N.Y.) and California as CA (not Ca.).

b) Do not abbreviate streets or states in the inside address (the address typed on the first page of a letter). Although this rule is often ignored, observing it gives letters a more elegant appearance.

c) Abbreviate compass points that *follow* street names.

Porter Street NW or Porter Street, NW

d) Spell out compass points that precede street names.

1500 South H Street
One North Broadway

40 Abbreviate social titles (*Ms., Mrs., Mr.*).

Ms. is now an accepted title, comparable to *Mr.* in that it does not indicate marital status. *Ms.* may be used in both business and social contexts; however, use *Miss* or *Mrs.* when you know that an individual prefers it.

The formal plural of the abbreviation *Mr.* is *Messrs.* and of *Mrs.* is *Mmes.* Abbreviate other titles only when you use the person's full name.

Gen. George S. Patton
Rev. Billy Graham
Gov. Peter Stuyvesant

If the full name is not used, do not abbreviate the title (General Patton, *not* Gen. Patton).

41 In general, abbreviate dates only in informal writing.

Dec. 7, 1941

With partial dates and in formal usage, write dates in full.

December 7, *not* Dec. 7

42 Use the *'s* to form the plural of an abbreviation that has one or more periods.

> Seventy-three M.D.'s attended the meeting.

43 Abbreviate *United States* when it is used as an adjective.

> U.S. foreign policy

Write out *United States* when it is used as a noun.

> The United States was represented by Vice President Martinez.

44 Observe the following usages in footnotes or parenthetical matter.

Abbreviate foreign words only when they appear in footnotes or parentheses. Since many people are not familiar with the foreign words from which their abbreviations are derived, the shortened versions may be a confusing jumble of letters. They are often incorrectly punctuated as well. You avoid such problems by writing out *for example, that is,* and *namely* when they appear in text. Be sure to separate them from what follows with a comma.

Replace	with
e.g.	for example
i.e.	that is
viz.	namely

Abbreviate the word *figure* only in a caption or parenthetical reference (fig. 1).

Capitalization

People sometimes write with all capital letters. That way, they don't have to bother with rules; in fact, they don't even have to shift from lower- to uppercase and back again. But text written entirely in capitals is hard to read. This shifts the burden to the reader, whose lot the writer should be trying to make easier, not harder. What's more, emphasis is lost when everything is emphasized. Which of the following gets the idea across better?

I SAID "NO!"   *or*   I said "NO!"

All capitals is a sloppy habit that should be abandoned. Instead, use capitalization as a flexible instrument of style to show emphasis or to indicate proper nouns.

45 **Capitalize the first word after a colon in the following cases:**

a) if the material following the colon is a formal rule or a complete statement that expresses the main thought

> The company has a new policy: Every employee is given a company car.

b) if what precedes the colon is a word like *Note* or *Caution*

> Caution: Radioactive material enclosed.

46 **Capitalize titles as follows:**

a) In titles of books, plays, television programs, etc., capitalize the first and last words, plus all principal words.

Articles, conjunctions, and short prepositions are not capitalized unless they begin the title. Prepositions are capitalized if they consist of four or more letters or if they are connected with a preceding verb.

Stop the World, I Want to Get Off
Customers Held Up by Gunmen
Situation Calls for Action
Peace Through Negotiations

b) Capitalize both parts of a hyphenated word in a title or headline unless it is considered as one word or is a compound numeral.

Well-Known Actor Dies
Anti-inflation Measures Taken
Report of the Ninety-fifth Congressional District

c) Capitalize personal titles only if they precede the name and are not separated by a comma.

Professor Reynolds
the treasurer, Will Knott
President Baker

47 Capitalize both full and shortened names of government agencies, bureaus, departments, or services.

California Dept. of Corporations, *or* Dept. of
    Corporations
U.S. Treasury Department, *or* Treasury Department
Library of Congress
Board of Supervisors
Highway Commission
Justice Department

Do not capitalize the words *government, federal, administration,* etc., except when part of the title of a specific entity.

> The U.S. Government is the largest employer in the nation.

> She hopes to work for the federal government.

Capitalization of departments or divisions of a company is optional.

> Claims Department, *or* claims department
> Engineering Division, *or* engineering division

48 **Capitalize points of the compass and regional terms when they refer to specific sections or when they are part of a precise descriptive title,**

the East	the Western Hemisphere
Eastern Europe	Chicago's South Side

but not when merely suggesting direction or position.

central states	south of town
east coast	northern lights
Middle Atlantic states	western Texas

Go west, young man. —John B. L. Soule

Go to the West, young man.

They moved to southern Illinois from the South.

49 **Capitalize abbreviations if the words they stand for are capitalized.**

M.D.   Ph.D.   M.P.   J.D.   Jr.

50 **Capitalize ethnic groups, factions, alliances, and political parties but not the word *party* unless it is part of the name:**

The New Party is a relative newcomer on the political scene.

The Democratic party will be the first to hold its convention.

He spoke for the Korean community.

Use lowercase for political groupings other than parties.

She represents the centrist faction of the Newspaper Guild.

But:

the Left, the Radical Right

Capitalize *African American* and *Caucasian*, but not *blacks*, *whites*, and slang words for the races.

51 **Capitalize captions and legends according to individual preference or in-house style.** In general, use lowercase for the words *figure*, *table*, and *plate* and their abbreviations when they appear in text.

> Please refer to figure 5.

> The chart below shows wages by skill level (fig. 5).

Capitalize *figure*, *table*, and *plate* when they appear in captions.

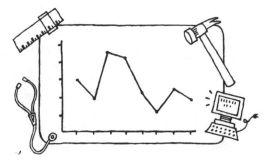

Fig. 5 – Wages by Skill Level

52 **Do not capitalize the seasons.**

> We always look forward to the fall colors.

53 **Capitalize time of day as follows:**

Use lowercase with periods (a.m. and p.m.) or small caps without periods (AM and PM).

Italics

Being able to print in italics is one of the joys of having a word processor or desktop publishing capabilities. When used correctly, italic type enhances the appearance of any document. If italic type is not available on your equipment, use underlining instead.

54 **Use italic type for titles of books, magazines, news-papers, and plays;** use roman type for titles of articles, chapters, poems, essays, and similar short works. (See Rule 28.)

New York Times	*Newsweek*
"Trees"	Chapter 12, "The Human Use of Human Beings"

55 **Italicize foreign words unless they are so widely used as to have become familiar.**

A black tie is *de rigeur* for the formal affair.

The plane was en route to Chicago when they heard the news.

56 **Use italics for emphasis—occasionally.**

Woman was God's *second* mistake.
—Friedrich Nietzsche

He was *audibly* tan. —Fran Lebowitz

57 Where words are referred to as words, numbers as numbers, and letters as letters, use italics to avoid confusion.

> The word *alright* should be written as two words, *all right*.

> Why is the word *tongue* feminine in Greek, Latin, Italian, Spanish, French, and German?
> —Austin O'Malley

> The *A's* should move to the front of the row.

58 Italicize short quotations when they stand alone, as at the beginning of a chapter. Use roman type and quotation marks when the quotation is incorporated into text. (See Rule 24.)

> As Mark Twain once said, "Put all your eggs in one basket—and watch that basket."

Never use both quotation marks and italics for the same material.

59 Italicize punctuation marks that immediately follow an italicized word.

> *Write Right!* is a handy reference.

60 Do not italicize the word *the* in the name of a newspaper unless it is part of the name.

> Does the library subscribe to the *Boston Globe* or *The Cleveland Plain Dealer*?

Numbers—Figures or Words?

Consistently observing a few conventions regarding numbers adds polish to writing.

61 **Spell out numbers in the following cases:**

a) at the beginning of a sentence

> *Three hours a day will produce as much as a man ought to write.* —Anthony Trollope

b) in whole numbers from one through nine and multiples such as *one hundred* and *three million*^{*}

> *Sometimes I've believed as many as six impossible things before breakfast.* —Lewis Carroll

c) in round numbers of indefinite expressions

  several thousand people
  the Roaring Twenties
  between two and three hundred employees
  in her eighties

d) in fractions standing alone or followed by *of a* or *of an*

  one-fourth inch   two-thirds of a cup
  two one-hundredths   one-half of an apple

e) preceding a unit modifier that contains a figure

  three 8-foot planks   six ½-inch strips

---

* I have adopted here the convention widely used in business and journalism. *The Chicago Manual of Style* suggests spelling out whole numbers between one and ninety-nine.

62 Use figures to represent numbers in the following cases:

a) when the number itself is 10 or more

b) when numbers below 10 occur with larger numbers and refer to the same general subject

> I have ordered 9 cups of coffee, 6 cups of tea, and 15 sandwiches to be delivered in one hour.

(The number *one* in "one hour" is not related to the other numbers and thus is not written as a figure.)

c) when they refer to parts of a book

> chapter 9   page 75
> figure 5   table 1

d) when they precede units of time, measurement, or money

> 18 years old   2 x 4 inches
> 9 o'clock or 9:00 $4 million
> $1.50   ¼-inch pipe
> 75¢   10 yards
> 3 hours 30 minutes 12 seconds

Note: Units of time, measurement, and money do not affect the rule determining use of figures when numbers appear elsewhere in the sentence. (See 62b.)

Wrong: The 3 students collected $50 apiece.
Right: The three students collected $50 apiece.

Spelling

I'm not very good at it myself, but the first rule about spelling is that there is only one z in is.
—George S. Kaufman

Misspelled words sometimes mislead and confuse; they also suggest carelessness and reflect poorly on the writer. Although spellcheckers have reduced the need for knowing how words are spelled, they do have shortcomings. The following verse from the *Journal of Irreproducible Results* illustrates my point. (I found 24 errors—how many can you find?)

> I have a spelling checker
> It came with my PC;
> It plainly makes four my revue
> Mistakes I cannot sea.
>
> I've run this poem threw it,
> I'm sure your pleased to no,
> Its letter perfect in it's weigh,
> My checker tolled me sew.
>
> Two rite with care is quite a feet
> Of witch won should bee proud,
> And wee mussed dew the best wee can,
> Sew flaws are knot aloud.

I often hear people lament "I can't spell," as if they were speaking of a genetic disorder. Being a poor speller is neither something to be proud of nor a permanent condition to which one must be resigned. Despite what legions of bad spellers would have us believe, English is a reasonably orderly language. Familiarity with a few rules is all that many people need to improve their spelling; the books listed in the Bibliography can also be helpful.

The most enjoyable way to improve spelling is to read good books—lots of them. Be alert to the appearance of words as you read, and consider the dictionary your ally in becoming acquainted with our rich language.

The person writing the copy for this ad should have made use of the dictionary!

63 Form plurals as follows:

a) if the noun ends in *o*

when preceded by a vowel, **always** add *s*

studios	cameos
kangaroos	patios
rodeos	zoos

when preceded by a consonant, **usually** add *es*

potatoes	innuendoes
heroes	torpedoes

but when a musical term, add only *s*

| solos | pianos |
| banjos | sextos |

Exceptions: mementos, zeros, avocados, plus about 40 more. If in doubt, consult your dictionary.

b) if the noun ends in *s, x, ch, sh,* or *z,* add *es*

| boxes | beaches |
| bushes | bosses |

c) if the noun ends in y

when preceded by a consonant, change the *y* to *i* and add *es*

company	companies
authority	authorities
category	categories
parody	parodies

when preceded by a vowel, simply add *s*

| attorney | attorneys |
| turkey | turkeys |

d) if it is a compound word

Form plurals with the principal word

notaries public	mothers-in-law
attorneys general	major generals
deputy chiefs of staff	commanders in chief
passers-by	by-products

Nouns ending with *-ful,* add *s* to the end of the word,

| cupfuls | teaspoonfuls |

unless you wish to convey the use of more than one container. In that case, write as two words and make the noun plural.

cups full (separate cups)
buckets full (separate buckets)

(See Rule 1d regarding possessives of compound words.)

e) acronyms, numbers, and letters

As much as possible without creating confusion, simply add *s* to form plurals.

VIPs	the three Rs
in twos and threes	the late 1960s

Use *'s* with lowercase letters or abbreviations with periods.

I.O.U.'s	x's and y's

Note: Errors are often made with the singular forms of *criteria*, *media*, and *phenomena*. If you are writing about only one, use the singular form of the words: *criterion*, *medium*, or *phenomenon*. For example, if you are enunciating only one standard or rule by which a judgment can be made, use *criterion*; for more than one, use *criteria*.

> The sole *criterion* for selection is punctuality. Content and appearance are the *criteria* on which the entries will be judged.

The word *data* is now widely used as a singular word in nonscientific writing; in formal and scientific writing, however, you should treat it as the plural word it is (data *are*, not data *is*).

---

f) foreign words

Certain words (primarily Latin in origin) form plurals according to their foreign derivation. Some of the most common are listed below, followed by examples of foreign words whose plural forms have become Anglicized. A recent edition of a good dictionary is your best guide.

Singular	Plural
alumnus (masc.)	alumni (masc. *or* masc. and fem.)
alumna (fem.)	alumnae (fem.)
axis	axes
crisis	crises
criterion	criteria
datum	data
medium	media *or* mediums
memorandum	memoranda *or* memorandums (*not* memorandas)
nucleus	nuclei
phenomenon	phenomena
stimulus	stimuli
stratum	strata

Anglicized Plurals

antenna	antennas
appendix	appendixes
cactus	cactuses
formula	formulas
index	indexes (scientific, use *indices*)
prospectus	prospectuses

64 Add suffixes as follows:

Drop the silent *e* at the end of a word when adding a suffix that begins with a vowel:

age	aging	force	forcible
move	movable	route	routing
sale	salable	use	usage

Exceptions: mileage, hoeing, and words such as manageable or serviceable, where dropping the final *e* would produce a hard consonant.

Double the final consonant of the root word when all of the following conditions are met:

> suffix begins with a vowel:
> (commit*t*ed, regret*t*able, runn*i*ng)

> root word ends in a single consonant that is preceded by a single vowel:
> sw*im* (swimming), gr*in* (grinning), fl*ap* (flapper)

> last syllable is accented, or the word consists of one syllable:
> remit (remitting), rip (ripped), put (putting)

Exceptions: chagrined, transferable

The following words do *not* meet at least one of the above requirements, and thus the final consonant is not doubled:

commit   commitment
> *(suffix does not begin with a vowel)*

appeal   appealed
> *(final consonant is preceded by a double vowel)*

travel   traveled
> *(last syllable is not accented)*

The following words *do* meet the requirements:

commit	committed
bag	baggage
red	reddish
occur	occurrence
refer	referred
transfer	transferred

Note: If the accent moves to the preceding syllable with the addition of a suffix, the final consonant is not doubled.

refer	reference
prefer	preference

65 Use the following guide for words ending in *-sede*, *-ceed*, and *-cede*.

Only one word ends in *-sede* (supersede), and three words end in *-ceed* (exceed, proceed, and succeed). All other words of this type end in *-cede* (precede, secede...).

Nothing succeeds like excess. —Oscar Wilde

66 Be careful of *ei* and *ie* words.

The grammar school jingle we learned has so many exceptions that you should use it only when you don't have a dictionary handy. The first line of the jingle is the most useful part.

Put *i* before *e*, except after *c*...
   (*i* before *e*): piece, brief, niece
   (except after *c*): receive, ceiling, deceive

This rule applies only when the words containing *ei* or *ie* are pronounced like *ee* (as in *need*). When the sound is other than *ee*, the correct spelling is usually *ei* (e.g., freight, neighbor, vein). Some exceptions are *either, neither, seize, financier,* and *weird.*

> *It is a pity that Chaucer, who had geneyus, was so unedicated. He's the wuss speller I know of.*
> —Artemus Ward

Word Division

Words that are divided at the right-hand margin are an interruption to the reader; incorrectly divided words slow the reader down even more. So divide words only when you must, and always do it correctly. Both parts of a divided word should be pronounceable, and you should avoid breaking a word so that the first fragment produces a misleading meaning (legis-lature, not leg-islature; thera-pist, not therapist).

67 **Divide words as follows:**

a) between syllables

num-ber	moun-tain
con-sum-er	vo-ca-tion
trou-sers	prod-uct
el-e-va-tor	west-ern
sher-iff	in-di-cate

Careful pronunciation or your dictionary will help you determine correct syllabification.

b) between double letters

quar-rel	refer-ring
com-mit-tee	ac-com-mo-date
op-pres-sion	flip-pant

unless the double letter comes at the end of the simple form of the word

call-ing	bless-ing
success-ful	add-ing
fluff-ier	hell-ish

c) in hyphenated words, only where the hyphen already exists

thirty-five, not thir-ty-five
sister-in-law, not sis-ter-in-law

d) at a prefix or suffix, but not within it

super-market, not su-permarket
contra-ceptive, not con-traceptive

e) to produce the most meaningful grouping

careless-ness, not care-lessness
consign-ment, not con-signment
re-arranged, not rear-ranged

f) after, not before, a one-letter syllable

bus*i*-ness	pol*i*-tics
sil*i*-con	stat*u*-ary

unless the one-letter syllable is part of the suffixes *-able* or *-ible*

illeg-ible	mov-able
inevit-able	permiss-ible

> *Note*: The *a* and *i* in many *-able* and *-ible* words are not one-letter syllables and should be divided as in the following examples:
>
> | | |
> |---|---|
> | ame-na-ble | pos-si-ble |
> | ter-ri-ble | char-i-ta-ble |
> | ca-pa-ble | swim-ma-ble |

68 Do *not* divide the following:

a) one-syllable words

b) words with fewer than six letters

c) one-letter syllables

   alone, not a-lone   eu-phoria, not euphori-a

d) two-letter syllables at the end of a word

   caller, not call-er   pur-chaser, not purchas-er
   walked, not walk-ed   leader, not lead-er

To state Rules 68c and d differently: Leave at least two letters before the hyphen and three letters after it.

e) these suffixes

-cial	-cion	-cious	-tious
-tial	-sion	-ceous	-geous
-sial	-tion	-gion	-gious

f) abbreviations, contractions, or a person's name

g) the last word of a paragraph or last word on a page

69 **When three or more consonants come together, let pronunciation be your guide.**

> punc-ture   match-ing
> chil-dren   birth-day

When in doubt, consult a dictionary, where you will find the words divided into syllables.

I saw a man on a horse with a wooden leg. See Rule 73, Misplaced Modifiers, p. 81.

Grammatical Guidelines

Agreement of Subject and Verb   70

Agreement of Subject and Pronoun   78

Parallel Construction   80

Misplaced Modifiers   81

Dangling Modifiers   82

Double Negatives   83

Reviewing Some Grammatical Terms   84

Grammatical Guidelines

For many people, the subject of grammar evokes images of a strict high school teacher who made life miserable by requiring them to diagram sentences. It seems unlikely to them that grammar might actually be useful. But grammar is one way of introducing order into our language. By making subjects and verbs agree, placing modifiers so as to avoid confusion, and so on, grammar helps us use language in a logical way. Communication proceeds more smoothly when we abide by these rules.

One of the best ways to get a grip on grammar is to develop an ear for the sound of properly used language. However, since many who speak on radio and television are among the worst language abusers, the visual act of reading good prose may be a better way of exposing yourself to the "sound" of correct grammar. Read widely and read the best writers. You will absorb grammar and style without even thinking about it.

> *Literature is simply the appropriate use of language.*
> —Evelyn Waugh

If you need to brush up on terminology, you will find a brief review at the end of this chapter. If you are already comfortable with nouns and verbs, subjects and predicates, and the concept of person, just sail right in.

70 **Make subject and verb agree both in person and number.**

> *Agreement is as pleasant in prose as it is in personal relations, and no more difficult to work for.*
> —Jacques Barzun

Errors in agreement are among the most common mistakes writers make. On the surface, the rule seems simple; a singular subject requires a singular verb: Tom is late.

A plural or compound subject requires a plural verb: Tom and Bill are late.

A subject in the first person requires a verb in the first person: *I am* ecstatic. A subject in the third person requires a verb in the third person: *She is* ecstatic.

However, applying this rule can be difficult. For example, it is not always clear which word or phrase is the subject or whether it is singular or plural. The most common difficulties regarding agreement of subject and verb are presented below in those two general categories: identifying the subject, and determining the number.

a) Identifying the Subject

(1) Intervening Phrases

Phrases that come between subject and verb do not affect the number of the verb.

> <u>Identification</u> of these compounds <u>has</u> remained difficult.

> The company's total <u>salaries</u>, exclusive of overtime, <u>are</u> $5,000 per week.

> <u>One</u> in five public water systems <u>contains</u> toxic substances.

> *<u>Horse sense</u> is what a horse has that <u>keeps</u> him from betting on people.* —W.C. Fields

The subjects of the above sentences are *identification, salaries, one* and *horse sense.* By mentally leaving out the phrases that come between those subjects and their verbs, you can determine whether a singular or plural verb is required.

(2) Phrases and Clauses as Subjects

When the subject of a sentence is a phrase or clause, it takes a singular verb. In the following sentences, the subjects are *What this country needs* and *The best way to keep your friends.*

> *<u>What this country needs</u> <u>is</u> a good 5¢ nickel.*
> —F.P. Adams

> *<u>The best way to keep your friends</u> <u>is</u> not to give them away.* —Wilson Mizner

(3) Inverted Order of Subject and Verb

The subject usually precedes the verb, but when it follows,

you may have trouble telling whether the verb should be singular or plural. In the following example, since the subject is *Linus Pauling*, not *Nobel Prize winners*, a singular verb is correct.

> Leading the list of Nobel Prize winners <u>was</u> <u>Linus Pauling</u>.

In the following sentence, *a group of taxpayers and their congressman* is a compound subject requiring a plural verb.

> Seeking to defeat the proposition <u>were</u> <u>a group of</u> <u>taxpayers and their congressman</u>.

If you first locate the subject, you will then know what the number of the verb should be.

b) Determining the Number

(1) Compound Subjects

Two subjects joined by *and* are a compound subject; they require a plural verb.

> The <u>title and abstract</u> of the report <u>are printed</u> on the first page.

> <u>Writing a report and submitting it for review</u> <u>are</u> difficult tasks for the new manager.

> <u>Motherhood and apple pie</u> <u>are endowed</u> with special virtues in the U.S.

Exceptions: If the two parts of the compound subject are regarded as one unit or refer to the same person or thing, use a singular verb.

> <u>Bacon and eggs is</u> a standard breakfast in some parts of the country

> <u>My friend and former classmate is</u> coming for a visit.

Compound subjects preceded by *each* or *every* are singular.

> <u>Every man, woman, and child is</u> given full consideration.

> <u>Each nut and bolt is</u> individually wrapped.

Company names, though they may combine several units or names, are considered as a single entity and thus take a singular verb.

> <u>Temple & Associates specializes</u> in psychological testing.

> <u>Charles Schwab & Company is</u> a discount broker.

(2) Collective Nouns

Nouns such as *family, couple, group, people, majority, percent,* and *personnel* take either singular or plural verbs.

- If the word refers to the group as a whole, or if the idea of oneness predominates, use a singular verb.

   The group is meeting tonight at seven.

   The elderly couple was the last to arrive.

A minority may be right; a majority is always wrong.
—Henrik Ibsen

- If the word refers to individuals or items within a group, use a plural verb.

    A group of nineteenth century paintings and statues were donated to the museum.

    A couple of latecomers were escorted to their seats.

- Some words take either singular or plural verbs, depending on how they are used.

    Human rights is a sensitive issue. (singular)

    Human rights are often ignored. (plural)

    Statistics is a difficult subject. (singular)

    The statistics show a decreasing birth rate. (plural)

Use singular verbs with nouns that are plural in form but singular in meaning, such as *politics, measles, checkers.*

    Measles is a preventable disease.

    Politics is perhaps the only profession for which no preparation is thought necessary.
    —Robert Louis Stevenson

The word *number* is singular when preceded by *the* and plural when preceded by *a.*

    A *number* of stock market indicators *were* favorable.

    The number of students enrolling *is* decreasing.

(3) Indefinite pronouns

The following pronouns are always singular: *another, each, every, either, neither,* and *one,* as are the compound pronouns made with *any, every, some,* and *no: anybody, anything, anyone, nobody, nothing, no one,* etc.

Neither of the tax returns *was* completed on time.

Each of you *is* welcome.

Every dog has his day. —Cervantes

When it is a question of money, everybody is of the same religion. —Voltaire

An expert is one who knows more and more about less and less. —Nicholas Murray Butler

---

Note: When the word *each* follows a plural subject, it does not affect the verb, which remains plural.

The voters each have their own opinion.

The following pronouns are always plural: *both, few, many, others,* and *several.*

> *Many are called, but few are chosen.*
> —Matthew 22:14

The following pronouns are either singular or plural, depending on how they are used: *all, none, any, some, more,* and *most.*

We've suffered some setbacks, but *all is* not lost. (singular)

The mistakes were not costly, but *all were* avoidable. (plural)

None of the laundry *was* properly cleaned. (singular)

Three people were in the plane, but *none were* hurt. (plural)

The relative pronouns *who, which,* and *that* are also either singular or plural, depending on whether the words they stand for (their antecedents) are singular or plural. In the expression "one of those who...," does *who* refer to *those* (which requires a plural verb) or to *one* (which requires a singular verb)? This appears to be an area in transition. Formal usage would designate *those* as the antecedent, making the plural verb the correct choice.

Formal: She is one of *those* who *follow* directions well.

In informal usage, *one* is considered the antecedent, and a singular verb is used.

Informal: She is *one* of those who *follows* directions well.

I suggest that you choose whichever sounds more natural in a given situation.

(4) Either...or, Neither...nor Constructions

When the elements connected by *either...or* or *neither ...nor* are singular, use a singular verb.

> Neither the address nor the signature was legible.

> *Neither snow, nor rain, nor heat, nor gloom of night stays these couriers from their appointed rounds.*
> —Herodotus

If the elements that are combined are plural, use a plural verb.

> Either personal checks or major credit cards are acceptable.

When the elements are both singular and plural, the number of the element immediately preceding the verb determines the number of the verb.

> Neither the twins nor their cousin is coming to the party.

Either war is obsolete or men are.
—Buckminster Fuller

This sometimes results in a sentence that is correct but awkward. If that happens, rewrite.

Awkward: Neither he nor I am willing to compromise.
Better: He is not willing to compromise, nor am I.

(5) Expressions of Time, Money, and Quantity

If a total amount is indicated, use a singular verb:

Ten dollars is a reasonable price.

If the reference is to individual units, use a plural verb:

Ten dollar bills are enclosed.

(6) Fractions

The number of the noun following a fraction determines the number of the verb:

Three-fourths of the ballots have been counted. (plural)

Three-fourths of the money is missing. (singular)

Democracy is the recurrent suspicion that more than half of the people are right more than half of the time. —E.B. White

71 Make subject and pronoun agree in number.

Just as subject and verb should agree in number, so should subject and pronoun agree.

The Democratic party has nominated its (not *their*) candidate.

EACH EMPLOYEE MUST PROVIDE

HIS or HER

THEIR

HIS

?

OWN EQUIPMENT.

Each employee provides his or her (not *their*) own tools.

More and more writers are looking for ways to avoid using the masculine pronouns (*he, him, his*) for both sexes. As a result, some have strayed from subject-pronoun agreement. They find a long history of such usage.

> *Everybody does and says what they please.*
> —Lord Byron

> *It's enough to drive anyone out of their senses.*
> —George Bernard Shaw

Often you can avoid both grammatical error and sexism by rewriting:

It's enough to drive you out of your senses.

The employees each provide their own tools.

72 Use parallel construction.

Express parallel thoughts in grammatically parallel terms. For example, a gerund should be paired with a gerund, an infinitive with an infinitive. In the first example below, the gerund *swimming* is paired with the infinitive *to ski*. In the correct example, two gerunds are used.

Wrong: Swimming is better exercise than to ski.
Right: Swimming is better exercise than skiing.

Wrong: They came on foot, by car, and bicycle.
Right: They came on foot, by car, and by bicycle.

Wrong: in spring, in summer, and fall
Right: in spring, in summer, and in fall *or*
in spring, summer, and fall

Use parallel construction in lists, outlines, or headings. If your list begins with strong verbs, make the entire list begin with such verbs. The following "Wrong" example (from the promotional brochure for a writing course!) switches from active verbs to passive nouns.

Wrong:

1. Add impact to every line
2. Explode writing myths
3. The simple techniques used to stimulate readers' interest

Right:

1. Add impact to every line
2. Explode writing myths
3. Use simple techniques to stimulate readers' interest

Use parallel words, phrases, clauses, verbs, and tenses to improve the flow of ideas and heighten impact. Similarity of form helps the reader recognize similarity of content or function.

> *We think according to nature; we speak according to rules; we act according to custom.* —Francis Bacon

> *...government of the people, by the people, and for the people.* —Abraham Lincoln

Parallel treatment also avoids the sexist implications of uneven handling of names.

Wrong: Mr. Swanson and Lydia

Right: George Swanson and Lydia Swanson; George and Lydia Swanson; George and Lydia

73 Avoid misplaced modifiers.

Keep related words together and in the order that conveys the intended meaning.

> We almost lost all of the crop.

> We lost almost all of the crop.

Both are correct grammatically, but only one accurately describes the actual situation. To avoid confusion, place adverbs directly *preceding* the word or phrase they modify.

Wrong: He told her that he wanted to marry her frequently.

Right: He frequently told her that he wanted to marry her.

Wrong: During the recession, she was an obvious candidate for dismissal in a hardly hit industry.

Right: During the recession, she was an obvious candidate for dismissal in an industry that was hit hard.

Sometimes slight rewording removes the confusion.

Wrong: The seminar is designed for adolescents who have been experimenting with drugs and their parents.

Right: The seminar is designed both for adolescents who have been experimenting with drugs and for their parents.

As the following examples illustrate, misplaced modifiers can produce some remarkable images, but your readers may be entertained at your expense.

I have discussed how to fill the empty containers with my employees.

The fire was extinguished before any damage was done by the Fire Department.

They saw a picture of an old woman hanging by the fireplace.

74 Avoid dangling modifiers.

A modifier "dangles" when what it modifies is missing or is misplaced in the sentence, as in *Strolling down the lane, the cottage came into view.* In such a sentence, the cottage appears to be doing the strolling. The sentence can be repaired in a number of ways. For example: *Strolling down the lane, I saw the cottage* or *As I strolled down the lane, the cottage came into view.*

Some danglers are so subtle that they slip by established writers and their editors. Others are real howlers.

At the age of five, his father died.

Being old and dog-eared, I was able to buy the book for a dollar.

Hidden in an antique seaman's chest, Aunt Keziah kept the damning evidence.

> *Exceptions:* Certain modifying phrases are so useful that they are accepted as correct even though they dangle. *All things considered, strictly speaking, judging by the record, curiously, admittedly,* and *assuming you're right* are examples of this well-established idiom.
>
> The word *hopefully* should be just as acceptable (as in *Hopefully, we will be on time*), but it is still frowned on by a few language mavens, and the *New York Times* style guide forbids its use as a dangler. You decide whether you want to stick with the *New York Times* or join the crowd of *hopefully* users. You can skirt the whole issue, as I do, by finding another way to express yourself.

75 In general, avoid double negatives.

Two words expressing negation tend to cancel each other and create a positive meaning, which may not be what the writer had in mind.

Wrong: The program is not going nowhere.
Right: The program is going nowhere.

Wrong: I couldn't scarcely believe what I heard.
Right: I could scarcely believe what I heard.

You may, however, choose a double negative for its subtle nuance of meaning (*The program is not without interest*), or for its humorous effect.

> *If people don't want to come out to the park, nobody's going to stop them.* —Yogi Berra
>
> *Let's forget it never happened.* —Ray Kass

Sometimes mistakes are made because the concept of negation doesn't use words like *no* or *not*.

Wrong: The absence of compassion was noticeably lacking.
Right: The absence of compassion was noticeable.
or   Compassion was lacking.

Avoid complicated negative constructions that burden the reader.

Poor: I couldn't see how it was not a disservice.
Better: I could see that it was a disservice.

Reviewing Some Grammatical Terms

Our review of the parts of speech begins with some brief definitions. Noun and verb head the list because of their importance; the remaining parts of speech are presented alphabetically. Next, we examine the parts of speech in action, as structural elements of a sentence (subjects, predicates, and so on). And finally, a table sorts out first, second, and third person.

Noun: A word that names a person, place, thing, quality, or act.

> *Life is not a spectacle or a feast; it is a predicament.*
> —George Santayana

Verb: A word that expresses action, mode of being, or occurrence.

> *Keep cool and collect.* —Mae West

When I <u>appear</u> in public, people <u>expect</u> me to <u>neigh</u>, <u>grind</u> my teeth, <u>paw</u> the ground, and <u>swish</u> my tail—none of which <u>is</u> easy. —Princess Anne

Adjective: A word or group of words that modifies (describes or limits) a noun or pronoun.

The <u>average</u>, <u>healthy</u>, <u>well-adjusted</u> adult gets up at 7:30 in the morning feeling just terrible. —Jean Kerr

(*average, healthy,* and *well-adjusted* modify *adult*)

Adverb: A word or group of words that modifies a verb, adjective, or other adverb.

I'd like to grow <u>very</u> old as <u>slowly</u> as possible. —Mayer Selznick

(*very* modifies the adjective *old; slowly* modifies the verb *grow*)

Conjunction: A word or group of words that connects other words or groups of words.

I'm a great believer in luck, <u>and</u> I find the harder I work, the more I have of it. —Thomas Jefferson

Preposition: A word or group of words that shows the relation between its object and some other word in the sentence; it often indicates position, motion, or direction. Examples are *of, from, against, with,* and *through.*

Idealism increases <u>in</u> direct proportion <u>to</u> one's distance <u>from</u> the problem. —John Galsworthy

Pronoun: A word that takes the place of a noun. Examples are *they, it, you, who,* and *she.*

<u>It</u>'s so beautifully arranged on the plate—<u>you</u> know someone's fingers have been all over <u>it</u>. —Julia Child

A given word can be a **noun,** an **adjective,** or a **verb;** how it is used in a sentence determines which role it performs.

They gathered around the *pool* table. (adjective)

Should we *pool* our resources? (verb)

The spilled water collected in a *pool.* (noun)

If we put the parts of speech to work in a sentence, they take on additional names: subject, predicate, object, complement, and modifier.

*The word **predicate** tends to disconcert twelve-year-olds, but it's less daunting when you look at it from your full height.* —Claire Kehrwald Cook

Subjects and **predicates** are the stripped-down basics of a sentence. A **simple predicate** is synonymous with **verb;** it tells what is predicated about (in other words, what is said about) the subject.

<u>Speed</u> <u>kills</u>.
SUBJECT   PREDICATE

In a more complicated sentence, the **complete predicate** includes not only the verb but its object, modifier, or complement. (See Glossary.)

<u>Speed</u> <u>kills those who throw caution to the winds.</u>
SUBJECT   COMPLETE PREDICATE

The **subject** of a sentence answers the question formed by putting *Who?* or *What?* <u>in front of</u> the verb.

(What kills?) <u>Speed</u> kills.
SUBJECT

The **direct object** of a sentence answers the question formed by putting the word *What?* or *Whom?* after the verb.

(I gave what?) I gave <u>money</u> to the worthy cause.
DIRECT OBJECT

(Thomasina loves whom?) Thomasina loves <u>Archibald</u>.

The **indirect object** receives the direct object.

I gave <u>John</u> money to pay the rent.
    INDIRECT OBJECT

Prepositions also have objects.

<u>between</u> the <u>sheets</u>   <u>under</u> the <u>bed</u>
PREPOSITION   OBJECT   PREPOSITION   OBJECT

Person: Person denotes the speaker (first person), the person spoken to (second person), or the person or thing spoken of (third person). Examples of the pronouns used for each person are as follows:

	Singular	**Plural**
First Person	I, me	we, us
Second Person	you	you
Third Person	he, she, it, him, her	they, them

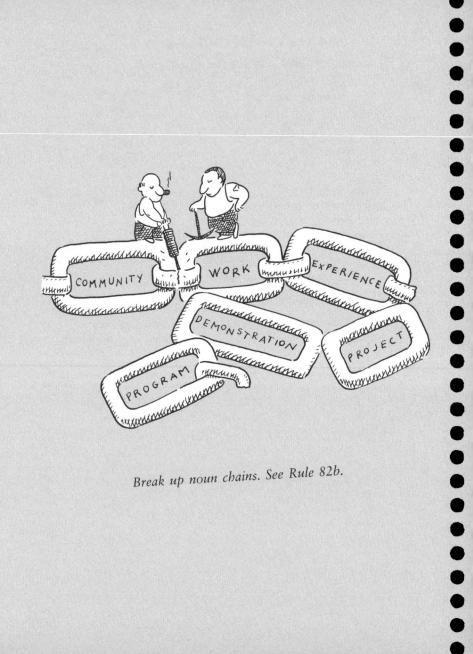

Break up noun chains. See Rule 82b.

Style

Omit Unnecessary Words   90

Prefer the Active Voice   93

Use a Positive Form   95

Be Specific and Concrete   95

Use Simple Words   96

Avoid Trendy Words and Clichés   97

Avoid Jargon   98

Vary Sentence Length and Type   100

Watch Out for the Word "Very"   101

Edit for Bias in Language   101

Look for Unintended Meanings   102

Style

Writing style is what makes one person's writing readable and another's tedious. Writing that draws attention to itself by being awkward or unnecessarily complicated detracts from the ideas it is intended to convey.

> *The greatest possible merit of style is, of course, to make the words absolutely disappear into the thought.* —Nathaniel Hawthorne

> *The fewer the words, and the more transparent they are, the easier they will be to understand.* —Jacques Barzun

76 Omit unnecessary words.

This rule is increasingly important because word processors encourage verbosity. However, the technology that spreads the disease also provides the cure; editing on a word processor is relatively simple.

Impressive writing does not derive from long words strung together in opaque sentences. If writing is hard to understand, it is not profound but merely poorly written.

Wordy: Our proposal follows the sequential itemization of points occurring elsewhere in your Request for Proposal, wherever possible, to facilitate your review.

Translation: We will follow your outline.

Redundancy and sloppy usage have been built into the language over the years. *General consensus of opinion* uses four words where only one is correct; *consensus* **means** collective opinion, or general agreement and accord.

Think about the meaning of a word. *Unanimous* means having agreement and consent of all; what is added by writing *completely unanimous*? Clutter. How about the ubiquitous *free gift*. Is there any other kind? If you write "Chances are...," you don't need to add "probably."

Wordy: Chances are that you have probably heard of...
Better: Chances are that you have heard of...
or   You have probably heard of...

> *Wherever we can make 25 words do the work of 50, we halve the area in which looseness and disorganization can flourish.* —Wilson Follett

To make 25 words do the work of 50, remove the unnecessary words from the following expressions.

hot water heater	join together
various different	refer back
current status	future plans
first time ever	past history
original founder	joint collaboration
regular routine	both men and women
limited only to	alike
unexpected surprise	ultimate outcome
sudden impulse	sum total
rarely ever	extra added features
small in size	advance warning
may possibly	temporary reprieve
present incumbent	10 a.m. Friday morning
two polar opposites	overused cliché

When you use the word "whether," omit "or not" if it is excess baggage.

Wordy: They couldn't decide whether or not to give all their money to charity.

Better: They couldn't decide whether to give all their money to charity.

In some cases "or not" is needed.

> *I figure you have the same chance of winning the lottery whether you play or not.* —Fran Lebowitz

"Rather" is redundant in a sentence with another comparative.

Wordy: It would be safer to destroy the chemicals rather than to store them.

Better: It would be safer to destroy the chemicals than to store them.

Omit unecessary prepositions.

    all of the details   = all the details

    finish up the work = finish the work

Leisurely openers like *There is, There are*, and *It is significant to note that* can usually be cut with no loss.

Wordy: There is some evidence that suggests...
Better: Some evidence suggests...

As well as is redundant when used with *both*.

Wordy: The press release was mailed both to employees as well as shareholders.

Better: The press release was mailed both to employees and shareholders.

Trim wordy expressions such as the following:

it is often the case that	= frequently
in the event that	= if
be of the opinion that	= believe
be in possession of	= have
owing to the fact that	= since or because
the fact that he had arrived	= his arrival
on the order of	= about
in advance of	= before
in spite of the fact that	= although
is indicative of	= indicates
had occasion to be	= was
put in an appearance	= appeared
take into consideration	= consider

The best cure for wordiness is to revise, revise, and revise again. Edit once strictly for spare words. When you think you have pruned every one (I almost wrote "pruned *out* every one"!), review your writing once more to see if you missed any.

> *He can compress the most words into the smallest idea of any man I ever met.* —Abraham Lincoln

> *The equivalent of junk food for the writer is redundancy, and the job of the editor is to count calories and impose diets.* —Bruce O. Boston

77 Prefer the active voice.

The difference between active and passive voice is the difference between *Karen read the report* and *The report was read by Karen.* In the active voice, the subject acts (*Karen read*) instead of being acted upon (*The report was read by...*).

The passive voice tends to use more words and often lacks the vigor of the active voice. Changing a sentence from passive to active usually improves it.

Passive: Hazardous reagents should never be poured into the sink.

Active: Never pour hazardous reagents into the sink.

Passive: The collision was witnessed by a pedestrian.

Active: A pedestrian witnessed the collision.

Passive constructions are appropriate in the following situations:

- when the thing acted upon is more important than the person performing the action,

    The meeting was canceled.

- in technical material,

    The test apparatus was divided into two zones.

- or where anonymity of those performing the action is appropriate.

    The information was leaked to the press.

Active

Passive

78 If appropriate, use a positive form.

Stating things positively often helps the reader get the right picture. Watch for the word *not* and see if you can restate the idea more effectively.

Negative: He often did not arrive on time.
Positive: He often arrived late.

Negative: The witness did not speak during the inquest.
Positive: The witness was silent during the inquest.

Replace:	with:
did not remember	forgot
was not present	was absent
did not pay attention to	ignored

Reserve the negative form for those instances where it produces the desired effect.

> *Of all noises, I think music is the least disagreeable.*
> —Samuel Johnson

> *I have always been in a condition in which I cannot* not *write.* —Barbara Tuchman

79 Be specific and concrete.

Bring abstract ideas down to earth with examples. Help your readers visualize what you're writing about by being specific.

Abstract: The equipment malfunctioned.
Concrete: The camera failed to expose any film.

Abstract: The new health and family programs improved employee performance.

Concrete: Absenteeism was reduced by 40% when the company built an employee gym and offered child-care services.

Wherever possible, replace abstract words with concrete ones:

Abstract:	Concrete:
vehicle	bicycle, panel truck
food	steak, papaya
color	red, chartreuse
emotion	hatred, confusion

80 Use simple words.

Why write "facilitate his departure" when you can write "help him leave"? Avoid four- or five-syllable words when one or two syllables convey the idea just as well.

Stilted: Per our aforementioned discussion, I am herewith enclosing a copy of...

Simple: As promised, here is a copy of...

> *I never write metropolis for seven cents because I can get the same price for city. I never write policeman because I can get the same money for cop.*
> —Mark Twain

Replace:	with:
utilize	use
ameliorate	improve
modification	change
deficiency	lack
preventative	preventive

Poor: I'll contact you to finalize the agreement.
Better: I'll call at your office to sign the contract.

81 Avoid trendy words and clichés.

> *Ready-made phrases are the prefabricated strips of words...that come crowding in when you do not want to take the trouble to think through what you are saying.* —George Orwell

The saturation provided by television, radio, and the various print media can turn a word into an instant cliché. *Paradigm, epiphany, bottom line, basically,* and *rocket scientist* have all joined the catalog of overused words. The best way to stifle these word fads is to avoid the popular word or phrase until it has had time to recuperate from overuse.

> *Anyone who uses the words "parameter" and "interface" should never be invited to a dinner party.* —Dick Cavett

82 Avoid jargon.

Jargon can be useful shorthand. Specialized vocabularies allow members of a professional group to communicate succinctly with other members of the group, but jargon has earned its bad reputation because it is often used simply to impress. Worse yet, it might be a smokescreen, burying truth rather than revealing it.

> *Jargon swamps thought.* —Jacques Barzun

Symptoms of everyday jargon include the following:

a) Interchangeable Parts of Speech

English is a remarkably adaptable language. It allows us to shuffle parts of speech, turning nouns into adjectives (*milk* carton), verbs into nouns (on the *mend*), nouns into verbs (to *face*), and adjectives into nouns (seeing *red*). Indeed, such flexibility is one of the strengths of our language.

However, when a better word is ignored in favor of an unnecessary coinage, our language becomes cluttered with such "verbs" as *to guest* and *to gift*. Nouns that have been pressed into service as verbs can create a breezy style. For example, if I was striving for a certain effect I might write "Let's front-page that story." But I would draw the line at such functional shifts as "I plan to Op-Ed my views in the Sunday paper" or "The investigator accessed the information in the public library." And when I find a chapter titled "How to Style Written English," I'm inclined to look for another handbook for advice on writing.

Find better ways of saying the following:

Poor: This model obsoletes all its predecessors.
Better: This model makes all its predecessors obsolete.

Poor: I'll reference that question to the legal staff.
Better: I'll refer that question to the legal staff.

b) Noun Chains

When nouns used as adjectives have slipped out of the writer's control, we find such impenetrable chains as *potassium permanganate-impregnated activated alumina medium*. Brevity was no doubt the motivation behind the creation of this chain of nouns, but clarity is lost. In any contest between brevity and clarity, clarity should always win.

Break up noun chains into manageable chunks. The above example could become *a medium of activated alumina that has been impregnated with potassium permanganate*.

Rewrite: *multimillion dollar data management equipment leasing industry*

    as: *a multimillion dollar industry that specializes in leasing equipment for data management.*

c) Bastard Words

Tacking *-ize* or *-wise* on the end of a legitimate word produces such illegitimate offspring as *enrollmentwise* and *strategize*. Some *-ize* words have won respectability (*computerize, idolize, harmonize*); even the much maligned *final-*

ize has some supporters who claim that alternatives like *complete, conclude, perfect,* or *terminate* do not carry the meaning of "to put into final form."

Be skeptical of those coined words. Do they accomplish anything? Is an established alternative at hand? Although some are useful, you avoid branding yourself as a jargoneer if you can find a satisfactory synonym.

83 Vary sentence length and type.

Retain reader interest by varying sentence length and by using different types of sentences. In all contexts other than instructions, a series of short declarative sentences becomes monotonous. Give your readers relief from the subject-verb-object order of most sentences by introducing variety.

Open with a subordinate clause:

> *If any man wishes to write a clear style, let him first be clear in his thoughts.* —Johann W. von Goethe

with an infinitive:

> *To get profit without risk, experience without danger, and reward without work, is as impossible as it is to live without being born.* —A. P. Gouthey

with a participial phrase:

> *Thrusting my nose firmly between his teeth, I threw him heavily to the ground on top of me.*
> —Mark Twain

with a preposition:

> *Behind the phony tinsel of Hollywood lies the real tinsel.* —Oscar Levant

Notice the rhythm of what you have written—is it choppy,

lively, flowing? Listen to the sound of the words—are there any awkward neighbors like "our products produced…"? Use rhythm, flow, and contrast to make language and meaning harmonious. Try reading out loud what you have written; it can reveal awkward passages and show where punctuation is needed.

84 Watch out for the word *very*.

The word *very* often signals sloppy writing. Overusing it weakens rather than intensifies your meaning.

Poor: His contribution was very critical.
Better: His contribution was critical.

Absolutes such as *unique* and *final* stand by themselves; do not attempt to make them more emphatic by adding the word *very*. If *very* seems necessary to strengthen your meaning, consider using another word that doesn't require buttressing.

Replace:	with:
very stubborn	obstinate, bullheaded
very weak	frail, feeble, fragile
very surprised	astonished, astounded, amazed

85 Edit for bias in language.

Bias-free language avoids possible offense. Many contemporary writers are able to find alternative terminology without resorting to awkward constructions. A few guidelines can help remove bias from your writing.

• Do not mention race, gender, age, or disability unless it is pertinent;

• Avoid stereotypes and labels that reveal a bias;

- Give parallel treatment (Mr. Waxman and Ms. Stone, not Mr. Waxman and Linda);
- Find substitutes for words that may be considered insensitive or confusing, such as masculine pronouns.

More detailed suggestions for avoiding bias can be found in two of my books, *Better Letters* and *Rewrite Right!* (see Bibliography).

86 Look for Unintended Meanings.

Pause and think about what you've written. In the heat of creation, you may have failed to notice that you've let something ridiculous slip by. Step back and take a fresh look in order to save yourself the embarrassment of sentences like the following—all of which appeared in print.

> No job losses are planned.

> Submit a list of all employees broken down by sex.

> No detail is too small to overlook.

> We feel pornography is an issue that demands a second look.

> In my attempt to kill a fly, I drove into a telephone pole.

> Dr. Ruth will talk about sex with Dick Cavett.

To make our words count for as much as possible is surely the simplest as well as the hardest secret of style.
—Wilson Follett

Confused & Abused Words

Advice, Advise
Affect, Effect
Allude, Refer
Allusion, Illusion
Alright
Alternate, Alternative
Ante, Anti
Anxious, Eager
Apt, Likely, Liable
Bad, Badly
Beside, Besides
Between, Among
Bi, Semi
Can, May
Capital, Capitol
Complement, Compliment
Comprise
Contact
Continual, Continuous
Convince, Persuade
Council, Counsel, Consul

Different from,
   Different than
Dilemma
Disburse, Disperse
Discreet, Discrete
Disinterested, Uninterested
Ecology
Emigrate, Immigrate
Eminent, Imminent
Enthused
Farther, Further
Fewer, Less
Flammable, Inflammable
Flaunt, Flout
Fulsome
Get, Got
Home, Hone
Hopefully
I, Me, Myself
Imply, Infer
Insure, Ensure, Assure

Irregardless
It's, Its
Lay, Lie
Lend, Loan
Like, As
Literally
Loose, Lose
Meantime, Meanwhile
Myself
Nauseated, Nauseous
People, Persons
Predominant, Predominate
Principle, Principal
Respectfully, Respectively

Shall, Will
Stanch, Staunch
Stationary, Stationery
Tenant, Tenet
That (adverbial)
That, Which
That, Who, Whose
Too
Was, Were
Who, Whom
Would of

Confused & Abused Words

For your born writer, nothing is so healing as the realization that he has come upon the right word.
—Catherine Drinker Bowen

Words are the writer's tools. A broad working vocabulary, rich in subtle shades of meaning, offers a better chance for the writer to choose "the right word." Wrong words are proliferating in the mass media. Not just typos, but the apparently conscious choice of the wrong word. Here are a few I found in a brief interval, together with the correct word:

    amble opportunity (ample)
    nerve-racking (-wracking)
    heart-rendering (-rending)
    free lays to the first 100 customers (leis)
    to whit (wit)
    reading from the scrip (script)
    honing in on the solution (homing in)
    inherits the reigns (reins)

If we use the wrong words, we not only impress the reader badly but we move our language in the direction of fewer choices. When years of blurring the distinction between such words as *disinterested* and *uninterested* have made the words interchangeable, we writers have fewer tools to work with.

The following list may help you find the right word.

Advice, Advise: The noun *advice* means suggestion or counsel; the verb *advise* means to give advice.

Affect, Effect: To sort out the confusion about these two words, remember that the most common use of *affect* is as a verb, and of *effect* is as a noun.

The verb *affect* means to influence or to have an effect on.

> The lawyer hoped to affect the jury's decision.

A less common meaning of *affect* as a verb is to pretend, to simulate or imitate in order to make a desired impression.

> The lawyer affected a look of disbelief when the defendant was unable to recall his whereabouts.

The noun *effect* means result or consequence.

> The lawyer's closing statement had an effect on the jury.

The verb *effect* means to bring about.

> The manager effected many changes in personnel.

Allude, Refer: To *allude* to something is to mention it indirectly, without identifying it specifically. To *refer* is to indicate directly.

> The speaker alluded to the hazards of smoking when he referred to the chart showing the incidence of lung cancer.

Allusion, Illusion: *Allusion*, the noun form of the verb *allude*, means an indirect reference to something not specifically identified, while *illusion* is a mistaken perception.

Alright: Although this word may eventually follow *already*, *altogether*, and *almost* into respectability, today it is still considered a misspelling of *all right*.

Alternate, Alternative: *Alternate* refers to every other one, or succeeding by turns; *alternative* strictly means one of two choices, although it is increasingly used for more than two choices. The distinction between these two words has been muddied by such usage as "alternate routes" and "alternate selections." Although the use of *alternate* to mean "offering a substitute" is too well established to be considered an

Alternate   *Alternative*

error, the best usage keeps *alternative* for "substitute" and *alternate* for "succeeding by turns."

Ante, Anti: *Ante-* means before or in front of. *Anti-* means against.

In the antebellum days, few Southerners were anti-slavery.

Anxious, Eager: Use *anxious* where there is a sense of anxiety, *eager* where there is pleasant expectation.

Apt, Liable, Likely: *Apt* implies a natural tendency (*I am apt to forget their names*). *Liable* suggests the possibility or probability of risk (*The theme of the ad campaign is liable to be misunderstood*). *Likely* conveys simple probability (*The forecast says rain is likely*).

Bad, Badly: To help you decide whether to use the adjective *bad* or the adverb *badly*, substitute a synonym in a sentence that calls for one or the other.

> I feel (*bad, badly*) about the incident.

Substitute *unhappy* and *unhappily*. Which fits? Clearly, you wouldn't write "I feel unhappily ..."; just so, you should not write "I feel badly about the incident."

Beside, Besides: When you mean *next to*, use *beside*; when you mean *in addition to* or *except for*, use *besides*.

> Besides the judge, no one was willing to sit beside the prisoner.

Between, Among: An ill-founded rule calls for using *between* with two items and *among* with more than two. Doggedly following this rule can lead you into such an absurdity as *She traveled among Santa Fe, Taos, and Albuquerque.* A better rule is to use *between* when individual relationships are emphasized and the number is unspecified (*he appeared between acts; cooperation between neighboring countries*), and when repetition is implied (*sobbing between each breath*). Use *among* with unspecified numbers if individual relationships are not emphasized (*discontent among the employees*). You are probably on safe ground using whichever word sounds right. The following examples illustrate choices that sound right.

> The anthropologist traveled among the Navajo and Hopi.

> She traveled between Santa Fe, Taos, and Albuquerque.

Bi, Semi: To minimize the confusion surrounding these two prefixes, use *bi-* in the sense of every two weeks (*biweekly*) or every two months (*bimonthly*); use *semi-* to mean twice each week (*semiweekly*), twice each month (*semimonthly*), and so on.

Can, May: The rule that distinguishes between *can* (the ability or power to do something) and *may* (permission to do it) is weakening. The Harper Dictionary of Contemporary Usage considers this "rather a pity, for the distinction is a nice one—and not really very hard to remember." Formal usage still requires the distinction, despite the prevalence of *can* for *may* in speech.

Capital, Capitol: *Capital* refers to wealth, the city that is the seat of government, or an uppercase letter. *Capitol* is the building in which state or federal officials congregate. The *Capitol*, when referring to the home of the U.S. Congress, is always capitalized.

capital
(money)

capitol
(building)

capital C
(upper case)

People who work in the Capitol disburse a great deal of the taxpayers' capital.

Complement, Compliment: *Complement* is both a verb and a noun, meaning to complete a whole or satisfy a need. *Compliment* also functions as both verb and noun, meaning praise.

> Her efforts complemented those of the rest of the team. (verb)

> A complement of 12 soldiers performed the assignment. (noun)

> She complimented him on the apple pie he had baked. (verb)

> Her compliment was sincere. (noun)

> *Nowadays we are all of us so hard up that the only pleasant things to pay are compliments.*
> —Oscar Wilde

Comprise: One of our most abused words, *comprise* means to include or be made up of; it is frequently confused with *compose* or incorrectly used as a synonym for *constitute*. The whole comprises the parts: the parts constitute the whole.

Wrong: High tech companies comprise only six percent of GNP.

Right: High tech companies constitute only six percent of GNP.

Right: The company comprises three divisions.

If you can substitute *include* for *comprise*, you are using *comprise* correctly.

Contact: Though widely accepted as a verb, *contact* is nonetheless an unsatisfactory choice if you can be more specific.

> I will phone you next week (or write, or drop by your office...).

Continual, Continuous: Dictionaries now list these words as synonymous, but maintaining the distinction between them helps preserve the richness of our vocabulary. *Continual* means over and over again; *continuous* means uninterrupted or unbroken.

> Since he coughed continually, the doctor kept him under continuous observation.

> *A man's memory may almost become the art of continually varying and misrepresenting his past, according to his interests in the present.*
> —George Santayana

Convince, Persuade: These words are synonymous, according to the *American Heritage Dictionary*; however, the correct choice to precede an infinitive is *persuade*.

> She persuaded me to attend the meeting.

> He convinced me of his sincerity.

Council, Counsel, Consul: *Council*, always a noun, refers to an assemblage of persons or a committee. *Counsel* has both verb and noun forms, meaning to advise, the advice itself, or an attorney.

> Counsel for the defense counseled the defense not to speak to the council members; the council resented his counsel.

Consul is a person in the foreign service of a country.

Different from, Different than: *Different from* is preferred when it is followed by a single noun, pronoun, or short phrase.

> His writing style is different from mine.

Different than is acceptable when it is followed by a clause or avoids wordiness.

Wordy: Writing style today is different from what it was a century ago.

Better: Writing style today is different than a century ago.

Dilemma: Reserve the use of *dilemma* for situations involving a choice between roughly equal alternatives; for general reference to difficult problems, use *predicament*.

Disburse, Disperse: *Disburse* means to pay out, as from a fund; *disperse* means to scatter.

> He disbursed the proceeds of the estate after he had dispersed the ashes.

Discreet, Discrete: *Discreet* is used to describe behavior that is prudent or respectful of propriety. *Discrete* frequently has a scientific connotation and means separate, distinct, or individual.

> He made discreet inquiries into her whereabouts.

> The smooth surface of water seems to contradict the discrete nature of its molecules.

Disinterested, Uninterested: Cautious writers still observe the distinction between these two words. *Disinterested* means objective or impartial, not influenced by personal advantage. *Uninterested* means indifferent or lacking interest in an outcome.

> A disinterested scientist is not uninterested in the outcome of his experiments.

Ecology: The study of the relationship between organisms and their environment. Often misused as a synonym for *environment*, which means surroundings.

Emigrate, Immigrate: To *emigrate* is to leave one's country permanently; thus one emigrates *from* a country. To *immi-*

grate is to move to a new country permanently; thus one immigrates *to* a country.

Eminent, Imminent: *Eminent* means well known or distinguished, while *imminent* means about to happen.

The arrival of the eminent statesman was imminent.

Enthused: A "back formation" from the word *enthusiasm* (as *donate* was derived from *donation*), *enthused* may never become acceptable in formal writing. Careful writers use *enthusiastic*.

Farther, Further: Traditional American usage calls for *farther* when actual physical distance is involved (*We walked farther than we had intended*) and when physical distance is only figurative (*The dispute is taking us farther apart*).

> *You can get much farther with a kind word and a gun than you can with a gun alone.* —Al Capone

Further is used in the sense of "more" or "additional" (*further deliberation, a further point*) and is increasingly used in the figurative sense of distance (*We are moving further from the truth*).

Fewer, Less: *Fewer* is used with individual items (fewer potatoes); *less* is used for quantity or bulk, when the item is regarded as a single entity (less oatmeal).

> The fewer mistakes you make, the less embarrassment you will feel.

> A diet that has less fat will also have fewer calories.

Less takes a singular noun and *fewer* a plural one, unless the plural is regarded as a single entity.

> I have less than ten dollars in my account.

Flammable, Inflammable: Both mean capable of burning. Because of the danger that *inflammable* will be mistaken for "not flammable," use *flammable* to mean combustible and *nonflammable* for its antonym.

Flaunt, Flout: A common error is to use *flaunt*, which means to show off, for *flout*, which means to show contempt. Although sometimes widespread errors evolve into acceptability, confusing these two words is simply an error.

> She flaunted her diamond tiara as a way of flouting her rival.

Fulsome: Modern usage limits the meaning of *fulsome* to offensively excessive or insincere; disgusting. This word is often used incorrectly to mean abundant or full. Don't write *fulsome praise* unless you wish to be uncomplimentary.

Get, Got: Although *get* and *got* can claim a long history of use in the English language, careful writers will avoid their casual overtones by substituting words such as *have* or *receive* whenever possible.

> I've got the answer. (I have...)

> We've got to comply. (We have to, We must...)

Home, Hone: The verb *hone*, meaning to sharpen, is sometimes incorrectly substituted for *home* in the expression *home in*, meaning to be guided to a target.

Wrong: He honed in on the objective.
Right: He honed his skills in order to earn a promotion.
Right: She homed in on the airport runway.

Hopefully: The word means full of hope (*He uttered his prayer hopefully and fervently*). The more common usage today is in place of "I hope" (*Hopefully, I will receive an answer today*). A great deal of ink has been spent trying to forestall acceptance of *hopefully* in the latter sense. But just as *happily, presumably,* and *luckily* have been accepted as standard usage, *hopefully* may someday cease to grate on the nerves of traditionalists. For now, a strong case can be made for avoiding the word simply because it is overworked.

I, Me, Myself: *I* is the subjective case and thus should be used when it is the subject of a sentence (the *who* or *what* that the rest of the sentence is about):

My brother and I went to the ball game.

Me is the objective case and should be used when it is the object of the action or thought conveyed by the verb of the sentence, or when it is the object of a preposition.

Between you and me, I hate Sunday afternoon football.

Ebenezer invited Elijah and me to the opera.

In a sentence such as the last, if you remove "Elijah and," it is obvious that *me* is the correct pronoun.

Myself is correctly used for emphasis (*I, myself, will see to it*) or as a reflexive (*I hurt myself falling off the roof*).

Do not use *myself* as a substitute for *I* or *me*.

Wrong: The money was given to my partner and myself.

Right: The money was given to my partner and me.

Wrong: My partner and myself are seeking underwriting for a business venture.

Right: My partner and I are seeking underwriting for a business venture.

Imply, Infer: To *imply* is to suggest directly or insinuate; to *infer* is to draw a conclusion or deduce.

> I infer from your remark that no threat was implied.

Insure, Ensure, Assure: All three words mean to make secure or certain.

> Victory is assured (or ensured, or insured).

Assure has the meaning of setting someone's mind at rest. Both *ensure* and *insure* mean to make secure from harm. Only *insure* should be used regarding guaranteeing of life or property against risk.

Irregardless: A redundancy. Use *regardless*.

It's, Its: *It's* is the contraction of *it is* or *it has*. *Its* is a possessive pronoun. (See Rule 1a.)

Lay, Lie: *Lay* is a transitive verb (i.e., it takes an object); it means to place or put down.

> Lay the package on the table.
> (*package* is the object of the verb *lay*)

Lie is an intransitive verb (i.e., it does not take an object); it means to recline. The past tense of *lie* is *lay*.

> Lie on your exercise mat.

> He lay on the mat for half an hour.

Lend, Loan: *Loan* used to be acceptable only as a noun (*I received a $1,000 loan*). But today *loan* used as a verb is widely accepted (*She loaned the museum three paintings*). Many writers, myself included, prefer to use *lend* when a verb is called for (*Lend me your pen*).

Like, As: *Like* is correct when used as a preposition.

> She writes like Hemingway.

In formal writing, do not use *like* as a conjunction; substitute *as* or *as if.*

> Residents of the model village live as the villagers did two hundred years ago.

> The shareholder spoke as if he planned to take over the company.

In journalism and informal writing, *like* is often used as a conjunction.

> Sales aren't growing like they were a decade ago.

> *Childbirth is like trying to push a grand piano through a transom.* —Alice Roosevelt Longworth

Literally: Although a *literal translation* is word for word and exact, *literally* has strayed into being used for emphasis in ways that are anything but literal. Your credibility is jeopardized if you write, *We were literally climbing the walls.* On the other hand, you might write *He literally got away with murder* and mean it if he killed someone and got away with it. Use *literally* with care.

Loose, Lose: *Loose* is an adjective meaning unrestrained or not fastened. *Lose* is a verb that is the antonym of *win* and *find.*

Meantime, Meanwhile: *Meantime* is a noun that refers to an interval between events.

> We will meet at 3:00 this afternoon. In the meantime, prepare your responses to the board's questions.

Meanwhile is an adverb meaning *during* the intervening time.

> Meanwhile, back at the ranch...

You can interchange *in the meantime* and *meanwhile*, but do not write *in the meanwhile*.

Myself: See I, Me, Myself, p. 115.

Nauseated, Nauseous: According to Theodore Bernstein, a person who feels sick is no more *nauseous* than a person who has been poisoned is *poisonous*. Though the distinction between the verb *nauseate* and the adjective *nauseous* has all but disappeared in speech, you should observe the difference in writing. Something that makes you feel sick is *nauseous* (*nauseous fumes*); what you feel is *nauseated* (*The fumes nauseated me*).

People, Persons: In general, use *people* for larger groups, *persons* for an exact or small number.

> Eight persons are being held as hostages.

> *The persons hardest to convince they're at the retirement age are children at bedtime.* —Shannon Fife

> *The trouble with people is not that they don't know but that they know so much that ain't so.*
> —Josh Billings

If *persons* sounds affected, try using a more specific noun, such as *commuters, residents,* or *visitors.*

Predominant, Predominate: *Predominant* is an adjective meaning most common or having the greatest influence or force. *Predominate* is a verb meaning to prevail or to have the greatest influence.

> The predominant theme of the parade was patriotism.

> The patriotic theme of the parade predominated over all others.

There is no such word as *predominately*.

Principal, Principle: *Principal* functions as both noun and adjective. The noun refers to the head of a school or firm, or to capital that earns interest; the adjective means chief or main. *Principle* is a noun meaning rule or standard.

> The principal's principal principle was *Be Prepared*.

Respectfully, Respectively: *Respectfully* means full of respect (*I respectfully disagree*). It may be used in the formal closing of a letter (*Respectfully yours*). *Respectively* means individually in the order given (*Suzanne Johnson and William Campbell were elected president and vice-president, respectively*). Do not sign a letter *Respectively yours*.

Shall, Will: This is one instance where the fading of an old grammatical distinction is welcome. Don't worry about rules regarding *shall* and *will*, or *should* and *would*. Just let your ear be your guide.

Stanch, Staunch: *Stanch* means to stop the flow; *staunch* is steadfast, true. You may need a *staunch* friend to *stanch* the flow of blood.

Stationary, Stationery: *Stationary* means fixed in position, not moving. *Stationery* is writing paper and envelopes. A good mnemonic is that *stationery* is what you need to write *letters*.

Tenant, Tenet: Although both words derive from Latin *tenere* (meaning to hold) and to the untrained ear may sound similar, the meanings of *tenant* and *tenet* do not overlap. A *tenant* is one who temporarily holds or occupies property (land, buildings). A *tenet* is an opinion or principle held by a person or organization.

> The tenants' association drew up a list of tenets for their organization.

That (adverbial): In the sense of "to that degree or amount," *that* is standard usage (*I won't buy a car that old*). But "I am not that hungry" is considered informal usage unless it is preceded by something that specifies how hungry "that hungry" is. For example, "John ate 12 pancakes, but I am not that hungry."

That, Which: Generally, use *that* to introduce restrictive, or defining, clauses; use *which* to introduce nonrestrictive clauses. (See Glossary.)

Restrictive: The pencil that needs sharpening is on my desk.

Nonrestrictive: The pencil, which needs sharpening, is on my desk.

In the restrictive example, the pencil is one of several and thus must be further identified. In the nonrestrictive example, there is only one pencil—and by the way, it needs sharpening.

In the following example, *which* might refer to the word *taxes* or to the entire preceding phrase.

> Any attempts to increase taxes, which would harm the recovery...

Rewrite to avoid such ambiguity.

> Any attempts to increase taxes that would harm the recovery...

or

> Since any attempts to increase taxes would harm the recovery...

Whenever you write *which*, try substituting *that*. If it fits, *that* is probably the better word to use.

That, Who, Whose: Although in earlier versions of *Write Right!* I observed that the rules governing the choice between *that* and *who* had been relaxed, I now think we've gone overboard. *That* threatens to obliterate *who*. Using *who* to refer to persons makes them seem more human, and we need all the help we can get in that direction these days. Use *that* to refer to things.

Poor: The students that met me in the classroom...
Better: The students who met me in the classroom...

Whose refers either to persons or things.

> The crowd, whose patience had worn thin, ...

> The building, whose architect won a national award, ...

Too: Sloppy use of the word *too* can create ambiguity or uncertainty. Is "I cannot recommend Sadie too highly" a plus or a minus for Sadie? One can't be sure. Though such use of *too* isn't exactly a double negative, it may be a negative-and-a-half. Remove confusion by writing "I heartily recommend Sadie," or "I have mixed feelings about Sadie"—whatever the case might be.

Wrong: The plan is too complicated. (How complicated is that?)
Right: The plan is too complicated to succeed.

Was, Were: Use *were* when expressing a wish or a condition contrary to fact and when following the words *as if* and *as though*.

> The silence made it seem as if he were speaking to an empty room.

> *If it were not for the presents, an elopement would be preferable.* —George Ade

Use *was* when expressing a past condition that is not contrary to fact.

> If Hortense was guilty, she did not show it.

Who, Whom: Feeling that the word sounds stilted, some writers have abandoned the use of *whom* everywhere except following a preposition (*To whom is it addressed?*). But it's still a good idea to know correct usage—if only to avoid such "hypercorrections" as "Whom do you think you are?"

The best guide for deciding whether to use *who* or *whom* is to substitute a personal pronoun. If *he, she,* or *they* would fit, use *who* (nominative case); if *him, her,* or *them* would fit, use *whom* (objective case).

The man who you thought committed the crime...
(you thought *he* committed the crime)

(Note: You could also omit *who* in the above example.)

To whom shall I report?
(to *him, her,* or *them*)

For prying into any human affairs, none are equal to those whom it does not concern. —Victor Hugo
(it does not concern *them*)

An acquaintance is a person whom we know well enough to borrow from, but not well enough to lend to. —Ambrose Bierce
(we know *him* well enough)

People who say they sleep like a baby usually don't have one. —Leo J. Burke
(*they* say)

He looks like a female llama who has just been startled in her bath.
—Winston Churchill (on Charles DeGaulle)
(*she* has just been startled)

Would of: Incorrect usage. Write *would have.*

I would have (*not* would of) been on time if I hadn't had a flat tire.

Appendix

Venolia's Reverse Rules for Writers   126

Glossary   128

Bibliography   140

Grammar Hotlines   142

Frequently Misspelled Words   143

Index   149

Venolia's Reverse Rules for Writers

Sometimes a tongue-in-cheek approach is effective in fixing a subject in our minds. In that spirit, I present the following summary of the subjects covered in *Write Right!*—plus a few not mentioned.

1. Put the apostrophe where its needed.

2. Never let a colon separate: the main parts of the sentence.

3. Avoid overuse, of commas.

4. Reserve the dash—which is often overused—for emphasis.

5. Avoid un-necessary hyphens; divide words only between sy-llables.

6. Use a semicolon where needed, use it properly; and never where not called for.

7. Avoid run-on sentences they seem to go on forever.

8. In general, don't abbrev.

9. Have a good reason for Capitalizing a word.

10. In formal writing, don't use contractions.

11. Consult a dictionery for correct spelling.

12. Observe the rule that verbs has to agree with their subjects.

13. Make each subject and pronoun agree in their number, too.

14. Use parallel construction in writing sentences, forming paragraphs, and to emphasize a point.

15. After studying these rules, dangling modifiers will be easy to correct.

16. Omit unnecessary, excess words that aren't needed.

17. Generally, writing should be in the active voice.

18. Don't use trendy words whose parameters are not viable.

19. Avoid verbing a noun.

20. The careful writer avoids bias in his words.

21. Watch out for irregular verbs that have crope into your language.

22. Eschew archaic words.

23. Proofread carefully in case you any words out.

24. When a writer has chosen a point of view, you should stick to it.

25. Mixing metaphors can be a real stroke of lightning.

26. No matter how hard you try, typos often silp by.

27. No double negatives are seldom inappropriate.

Glossary

Active Voice: The form of the verb used when the subject performs the action. (See Rule 77, p. 93.)

Adjective: Modifies (describes or limits) a noun or pronoun. It may be a single word, phrase, or clause.

> A _good_ politician is quite as unthinkable as an _honest_ burglar. —H. L. Mencken

Adverb: Modifies a verb, an adjective, or another adverb. May be a single word, phrase, or clause.

> The secret of dealing _successfully_ with a child is not to be its parent. —Mell Lazarus

A _conjunctive adverb_ connects clauses or sentences. See Conjunction.

> I tape, _therefore_ I am. —Studs Terkel

Antecedent: The word, phrase, or clause referred to by a pronoun. In the following example, the pronoun _it_ refers to _talent_; thus, _talent_ is the antecedent of _it_.

> Everyone has talent. What is rare is the courage to follow the _talent_ to the dark place where _it_ leads. —Erica Jong

Antonym: A word having a meaning opposite that of another word. _Spicy_ is the antonym of _bland_; _ill_ is the antonym of _healthy_.

Appositive: A word or phrase that is an explanatory equivalent of another word or phrase. Since they are nonrestrictive, they should be surrounded by commas. (See Rule 11c.)

> Stephen Foster, <u>the American composer</u>, was born in 1826.

> My uncle, <u>known affectionately as Smilin' Sam</u>, has a family story for every occasion.

Article: The words *a, an,* and *the.*

Case: The changes in form made in nouns or pronouns to reflect how they are used in a sentence. For example, the word *children* is changed to *children's* and the word *person* to *person's* to show possession. Nouns in English once had many case forms, but the only one is use today is the possessive. Pronouns, however, continue to change form to show their relation to the rest of the sentence. The three cases of pronouns are as follows:

(1) The *subjective* or *nominative* case is used when the pronoun is the subject of a verb.

> My partner and *I* started a new venture.
> (*I* is the subject of the verb *started*)

(2) The *objective* case is used when the pronoun is the object of a verb or preposition.

> The patent was awarded to my partner and *me.*
> (*me* is the object of the preposition *to*)

(3) The *possessive* case is used to show possession.

> The patent is *ours.*

Clause: A group of words that contains a subject and verb.

Coordinate clauses have the same rank and are connected by a coordinating conjunction.

> *The wise make proverbs and <u>fools repeat them</u>.*
> —Isaac D'Israeli

Dependent clauses (also known as subordinate) do not express a complete thought when standing alone.

> <u>*If you have a weak candidate and a weak platform,*</u> *wrap yourself in the American flag and talk about the Constitution.* —Matthew S. Quay

Independent clauses (also called principal or main) are those which would make sense by themselves.

> <u>*Old age isn't so bad*</u> *when you consider the alternative.* —Maurice Chevalier

Nonrestrictive clauses could be omitted without changing the meaning; they are surrounded by commas.

> *Practical men, <u>who believe themselves to be quite exempt from any intellectual influences</u>, are usually the slaves of some defunct economist.*
> —John Maynard Keynes

Restrictive clauses are essential to the meaning (i.e., could not be left out without changing the meaning of the sentence).

> *The man <u>who walks alone</u> is soon trailed by the F.B.I.* —Wright Morris

Cliché: An expression that has lost its freshness by being overused. Examples are *conspicuous by its absence, in the final analysis, add insult to injury, crying need,* and *it goes without saying.*

Comma Fault: The error in which a comma is the only punctuation between two independent clauses. Rewrite using a semicolon or making the second clause a separate sentence.

Wrong: The trial itself was televised, however, reporters were barred from the courtroom during jury selection.

Right: The trial itself was televised; however, reporters were barred from the courtroom during jury selection.

Wrong: Some sentences are too long, they should be broken up into more manageable chunks.

Right: Some sentences are too long. They should be broken up into more manageable chunks.

Complement: A word or phrase that completes the meaning of the verb.

> *Great artists need <u>great clients</u>.* —I. M. Pei

> *I owe <u>the public nothing</u>.* —J. P. Morgan

> *Information is <u>the currency of democracy</u>.*
> —Ralph Nader

Compound: Consisting of two or more elements.

A *compound adjective*, also known as a unit modifier, consists of two or more adjectives modifying the same noun.

> *That <u>swarming</u>, <u>million-footed</u>, <u>tower-masted</u>, and <u>sky-soaring</u> citadel that bears the name of the Island of Manhattan.* —Thomas Wolfe

A *compound sentence* consists of two or more independent clauses.

> *A little learning is a dangerous thing, but a lot of ignorance is just as bad.* —Bob Edwards

A *compound subject* consists of two or more subjects having the same verb.

> *Papa, potatoes, poultry, prunes, and prism are all very good words for the lips; especially prunes and prism.* —Charles Dickens

A *compound verb* consists of two or more verbs having the same subject. In the following example, *tore off* and *blew down* both have the same subject: *strong winds*.

> The strong winds <u>tore off</u> roofs and <u>blew down</u> power lines.

Conjunction: A single word or group of words that connects other words or groups of words. See Adverb, Conjunctive.

Coordinate conjunctions connect words, phrases, or clauses of equal rank; for example, *and, but, or, nor, for, however, moreover, then, therefore, yet, still, both/and, not only/but also, either/or, neither/nor.*

Subordinate conjunctions connect clauses of unequal rank (i.e., an independent and a dependent clause). Examples are *as, as if, because, if, since, that, till, unless, when, where, whether.*

Dangling Modifier: A modifier with an unclear reference. (See Rule 74.)

> <u>Having been buried in the attic for generations</u>, I was delighted to find the old manuscript.

Double Negative: Two negative words that cancel each other to create a positive meaning. Such usage is incorrect if it is unintended (*No one should go nowhere near the edge*), but correct if it is chosen for its subtle nuances (*No one should be unaware of the hazards*). Even so, a positive statement is often more effective (*Everyone should be aware of the hazards*). (See Rule 75.)

Gerund: The *-ing* form of a verb that serves as a noun.

> *Seeing* is *believing.*

> Does anyone object to my *smoking?*

(Note the possessive pronoun; "Does anyone object to *me* smoking?" would be incorrect.)

Idiom: Idiomatic expressions, such as *rubbing someone the wrong way*, do not conform to the logic of the language. Sometimes the meaning of the expression cannot be derived from the meaning of the individual words, as in the phrases *to take in* or *to make up for*. Occasionally their construction violates grammatical rules, as in the expression *Take it easy*. If we followed the grammatical rules governing adverbs, the expression would be *Take it easily*.

Infinitive: The form of a verb used with *to*.

> *Better <u>to remain</u> silent and be thought a fool than <u>to speak</u> out and remove all doubt.* —Abraham Lincoln

Split infinitives (words inserted between *to* and the verb) have long been an acceptable way to avoid awkward writing. Without split infinitives, Trekkies would be unable "to boldly go"!

> Feel free *to utterly disregard* this formerly steadfast rule.

Interjection: An exclamation, such as *Wow!* or *Heavens to Betsy!*

Misplaced Modifier: A modifier that gives a misleading meaning by being incorrectly placed in a sentence. (See Rule 73.)

> The mayor met informally to discuss food prices and the high cost of living with several women.

Nonrestrictive Elements: Words, phrases, or clauses that add information that is not essential to the meaning.

> Theobald Tompkins, who has been our neighbor for twenty years, is moving to Arizona next week.

Noun: A word that names a person, place, thing, quality, or act.

A *proper noun* names a specific person, place, or thing; it is capitalized.

> the Big Apple, Julius Caesar, Hallowe'en

Number: Changes made, such as adding an *s*, to reflect whether a word is singular or plural.

Singular: a porcupine

Plural: three porcupines

Object: The word or phrase that names the thing acted upon by the subject and verb. Objects are complements; they complete the meaning of the verb.

> She visited *the ancient cathedral*.

A *direct object* names the thing acted upon by the subject.

> I bought a *book*.

An *indirect object* receives whatever is named by the direct object.

> I bought *Aunt Hester* a book.

You can identify the direct object by following the subject and verb with the question "What?" I bought what? A book. You can identify the indirect object by asking *who* received whatever is named by the direct object. Who received the book? Aunt Hester.

Participle: A form of a verb that has some of the properties of an adjective and some of a verb. Like an adjective, it can modify a noun or pronoun; like a verb, it can take an object.

> *Success is <u>getting</u> what you want; happiness is <u>wanting</u> what you get.* —Charles F. Kettering

Glowing coals, *grayed* collars, *run-down* heels, and *whipped* cream are examples of verb forms that function as adjectives, and thus are participles.

Parts of Speech: Nouns, pronouns, verbs, adjectives, adverbs, prepositions, conjunctions, and interjections. In the days of *McGuffey's Reader*, students used to learn the parts of speech with the help of the following jingle:

> A NOUN's the name of anything;
> As, *school* or *garden, hoop* or *swing.*
>
> ADJECTIVES tell the kind of noun;
> As, *great, small, pretty, white,* or *brown.*
>
> Instead of nouns the PRONOUNS stand:
> *Their* heads, *your* face, *its* paw, *his* hand.

VERBS tell of something being done:
You *read, count, sing, laugh, jump,* or *run.*

How things are done the ADVERBS tell;
As, *slowly, quickly, ill,* or *well.*

CONJUNCTIONS join the words together;
As, men *and* women, wind *or* weather.

The PREPOSITION stands before
a noun; as, *in* or *through* a door.

The INTERJECTION shows surprise;
As, *Oh!* how pretty! *Ah!* how wise!

Passive Voice: The form of the verb used when the subject is the receiver of the action. (See Rule 77, p.93-94.)

Person: Person denotes the speaker (first person), the person spoken to (second person), or the person or thing spoken of (third person). (See p. 87.)

Possessive: Showing ownership; also known as the genitive case. See Case.

> *He is a sheep in* <u>*sheep's*</u> *clothing.*
> —Winston Churchill

Predicate: A group of words that makes a statement or asks a question about the subject of a sentence. A *simple predicate* consists of a verb (*can preach*, in the following example). A *complete predicate* includes verbs, modifiers, objects, and complements (*can preach a better sermon with your life than with your lips*).

> *You can preach a better sermon with your life than with your lips.* —Oliver Goldsmith

Prefix: A word element that is attached to the front of a root word and changes the meaning of the root: *dis*belief, *in*attentive.

Preposition: A word or group of words that shows the relation between its object and some other word in the sentence.

> Most hierarchies were established <u>by</u> men who now monopolize the upper levels, thus depriving women <u>of</u> their rightful share <u>of</u> opportunities <u>for</u> incompetence.
> —Laurence Peter

Perhaps no other rule of grammar has prompted so many to say so much as the now-outdated rule prohibiting ending a sentence with a preposition.

> The grammar has a rule absurd
> Which I would call an outworn myth:
> A preposition is a word
> You mustn't end a sentence with. —Berton Braley

> What this country needs is more free speech worth listening to. —Hansell B. Duckett

Pronoun: A word that represents or stands in for a noun.

Personal pronouns are *I, you, he, she, it, they,* and their inflected forms (*me, my, your, them,* etc.).

Possessive pronouns represent the possessor and the thing possessed.

> The book is *mine.*

Relative pronouns (*who, whom, which, that, what*) join subordinate clauses to their antecedents. In the following sentence, the relative pronoun *who* joins the clause *sang Irish folk songs* with the antecedent *girl.*

> The girl *who* sang Irish folk songs was the star of the show.

Restrictive Elements: Words, phrases, or clauses that are essential to the meaning.

> The joke *that gets the most laughs* wins the prize.

Sentence: A combination of words that contains at least one subject and predicate (grammatical definition); a group of words that expresses a complete thought (popular definition).

A *simple sentence* consists of subject and predicate; in other words, an independent clause.

> *Our national flower is the concrete cloverleaf.*
> —Lewis Mumford

A *compound sentence* consists of two or more independent clauses.

> *Life is a shipwreck, but we must not forget to sing in the lifeboats.* —Voltaire

A *complex sentence* consists of one independent clause and one or more dependent (subordinate) clauses; in the following example, the independent clause is underlined.

> <u>*New York is the only city in the world*</u> *where you can be deliberately run down on the sidewalk by a pedestrian.* —Russell Baker

Subject: The part of a sentence about which something is said.

> *Time* flies.

You can identify the subject by putting *what* or *who* in front of the verb; your answer to the question thus formed is the subject. (What flies? *Time* flies.)

> *Some <u>people</u> think <u>they</u> are worth a lot of money because <u>they</u> have it.* —Edmund Fuller

Subjective Case: Nominative case. See Case.

Subordinate Clause: See Clause, Dependent.

Suffix: A word element added to the end of a root or stem word and serving to make a new word or an inflected form of the word. Thus, *-ness* and *-ren* added to *gentle* and *child* create the new word *gentleness* and the inflected word *children*. Other examples of suffixes are mother*hood*, depend*able*, hilari*ous*, end*ed*, and walk*ing*.

Synonym: A word having a meaning identical with or very similar to that of another word. *Shout* is a synonym for *yell*; *likely* is a synonym for *probable*. See Antonym.

Unit Modifier: See Compound Adjective.

Verb: A word that expresses action, being, or occurrence. See Predicate.

> Time *flies*.

Voice: See Active Voice, Passive Voice.

Bibliography

Allen, Reginald E., *The Concise Oxford Dictionary of Current English*, London: Oxford University Press, 1990.

Boston, Bruce O., ed., *STET! Tricks of the Trade for Writers and Editors*, Alexandria, VA: Editorial Experts, Inc., 1986.

Chapman, Robert L., ed., *Roget's International Thesaurus*, 5th ed., New York: HarperCollins, 1992.

Cheney, Theodore A. Rees, *Getting the Words Right—How to Rewrite, Edit, Revise*, Cincinnati, OH: Writer's Digest Books, 1983.

Chicago Manual of Style, The, 14th ed., Chicago: University of Chicago Press, 1993.

Drummond, Val, *Grammar for Grownups: A Guide to Grammar & Usage for Everyone Who Has to Put Words on Paper Effectively*, New York: HarperPerennial, 1993.

Dusseau, John L., *Bugaboos, Chimeras, and Achilles' Heels: 10,001 Difficult Words and How to Use Them*, Englewood Cliffs, N.J.: Prentice Hall, Inc., 1993.

Economist Style Guide, The: The Essentials of Elegant Writing, Reading, MA: Addison-Wesley Publishing Co., 1992.

Evans, Bergen, *The Word-a-Day Vocabulary Builder*, revised and updated by Jess Stein, New York: Ballantine Books, 1981.

Follett, Wilson, *Modern American Usage*, New York: Avenel Books/Farrar, Straus & Giroux, Inc., 1980.

Gordon, Teri, *The Perfect Speller*, Stamford, CT: Longmeadow Press, 1992.

Gorrell, Donna, *A Writer's Handbook, from A to Z*, Needham Heights, MA: Allyn & Bacon, 1994.

Harrison, Gwen, *Vocabulary Dynamics*, New York: Warner Books, 1992.

Hopper, Vincent F., Cedric Gale, Ronald C. Foote, and Benjamin W. Griffith, *Essentials of English: A Practical Handbook of Grammar and Effective Writing Techniques*, 4th ed., Hauppauge, NY: Barron's Educational Series, 1990.

Mager, N. H., and S. K. Mager, *Encyclopedic Dictionary of English Usage*, 2nd ed., revised by John Domini, Englewood Cliffs, NJ: Prentice Hall, 1993.

Merriam-Webster's Secretarial Handbook, 3rd ed., Springfield, MA: G. & C. Merriam Co., 1993.

Miller, Casey and Kate Swift, *The Handbook of Nonsexist Writing*, New York: HarperCollins, 1988.

Murray, Donald, *Writing for Your Readers: Notes on the Writer's Craft from the Boston Globe*, 2nd ed., Chester, CT: Globe Pequot, 1992.

Osborn, Patricia, *How Grammar Works—A Self-Teaching Guide*, New York: John Wiley & Sons, Inc., 1989.

Parker, Roger C., *Looking Good in Print*, 2nd ed., Alexandria, VA: Tools of the Trade, 1992.

Sabin, William, A., *The Gregg Reference Manual*, 7th ed., Glencoe, IL: Gregg Division/McGraw-Hill Book Co., 1992.

Shaw, Harry, *Errors in English and Ways to Correct Them*, New York: Harper Perennial, 1993.

_____, *Punctuate It Right!*, 2nd ed., New York: HarperCollins, 1993.

Swan, Michael, *Practical English Usage*, London: Oxford University Press, 1980.

Tarrant, John, *Business Writing with Style: Strategies for Success,* New York: John Wiley, 1991.

Tarshis, Barry, *Grammar for Smart People: Your User-Friendly Guide to Speaking and Writing Better English,* New York: Pocket Books, 1992.

Turabian, Kate L., *A Manual for Writers of Term Papers, Theses, and Dissertations,* 5th ed., Chicago: University of Chicago Press, 1987.

Venolia, Jan, *Rewrite Right! How to Revise Your Way to Better Writing,* Berkeley, CA: Ten Speed Press, 1987.

————, *Better Letters: A Handbook of Business and Personal Correspondence,* Berkeley, CA: Ten Speed Press, 1982.

Weiner, Ed, *Desktop Publishing Made Simple,* Garden City, NY: Doubleday, 1991.

Grammar Hotlines

A number of colleges in the United States and Canada operate Grammar Hotlines. Staffed by graduate students, faculty members, and retired teachers, these hotlines will answer short questions about writing, grammar, punctuation, spelling, diction, and syntax. For a free copy of the Grammar Hotline Directory, send a self-addressed stamped No. 10 envelope (business size) to:

> Grammar Hotline Directory
> Tidewater Community College Writing Center
> 1700 College Crescent
> Virginia Beach, VA 23456

The directory is updated each January.

Frequently Misspelled Words

Note: The following list contains several pairs of "sound-alikes." A brief definition (in parenthesis) identifies the first of the sound-alike words; the second sound-alike (indented) is defined at its alphabetical entry.

A

aberration
abridgment
absence
accelerator
accept (receive)
   except
accessible
accessory
accommodate
accumulate
achievement
acknowledgment
acquiesce
acquittal
adjourn
adolescence
advertisement
aerosol
affidavit
aging

algorithm
align
allotment
allotted
all right
already
anachronism
analogous
analysis
ancillary
anesthetic
annihilate
anomaly
anonymous
antecedent
antihistamine
apartheid
aperture
apparatus
apparel
appraisal
apropos

arctic
arraign
arteriosclerosis
arthritis
asphyxiate
aspirin
assessor
asterisk
attendance
attorneys
autumn
auxiliary

B

balance
ballistic
balloon
bankruptcy
barbiturate
basically
beneficiary

benign
bereave
bilateral
bilingual
binary
biodegradable
biopsy
bipartisan
blatant
bloc (group)
bouillon (soup)
    bullion
bourgeois
boutique
boycott
braille
brief
bruise
bullion (gold)
    bouillon
bureaucracy
business
byte

C

caffeine
calendar
calorie
campaign
cannot
captain
carat
carbohydrate
carburetor
Caribbean

carriage
Caucasian
caucus
caveat
ceiling
cellar
cemetery
censor
census
centimeter
centrifugal
cerebral
certain
changeable
charisma
chassis
chauvinist
chiropractor
chlorophyll
chocolate
cholesterol
Christian
Cincinnati
cipher
circuit
cite (quote)
    sight
    site
clothes
cocaine
coliseum
    (or colosseum)
collar
collateral
colonel
colossal

column
commitment
commodities
compatible
competent
concurrence
condemn
conductor
conduit
conjugal
Connecticut
conscience
consensus
consortium
continuum
corps
correspondence
counterfeit
coup d'état
courtesy
cousin
cryptic
curtain
cylinder
czar

D

database
debugging
deceive
decibel
deductible
defendant
deferred
depot

depreciate
descend
desiccate
desperate
deterrent
develop
diaphragm
dichotomy
dictionary
diesel
digital
dilemma
dinosaur
disappear
disappoint
disburse (pay out)
   diperse
discreet (cautious)
discrete (separate)
disperse (scatter)
   disburse
dissipate
distributor
doubt
dyeing (coloring)
dying (death)

E

ecstasy
eighth
either
elicit (draw forth)
   illicit
embarrass
emphysema

empirical
encyclopedia
endeavor
entrepreneur
envelope
epitome
equipped
equity
equivocal
errata
erroneous
esthetic
   (or aesthetic)
euthanasia
exaggerate
except
   (other than)
   accept
exhaust
exhibition
exhilarate
existential
exponential
extraterrestrial

F

facsimile
familiar
faze (disturb)
   phase
feasibility
feature
February
fetus
fiduciary

fierce
flourish
fluorescent
fluoridate
foreign
foreseeable
foreword
forfeit
freight
fulfill

G

gallon
gauge
genealogy
generic
geriatrics
gestalt
ghetto
gourmet
governor
graffiti
grammar
grief
grievance
guarantee
guerrilla
   (or guerilla)
guess
gynecology

H

hallucinogen
harass

Hawaiian
height
heir
hemorrhage
hertz
hiatus
hierarchy
holistic
holocaust
homogeneous
hors d'oeuvre
hydraulic
hygiene
hypocrisy

I

idiosyncrasy
idle (inactive)
idol (image)
illicit (forbidden)
   elicit
impeccable
impetus
impresario
imprimatur
inadvertent
incessant
incumbent
independent
indictment
indispensable
infrared
innocuous
innuendo
inoculate

intermittent
intravenous
iridescent
irrelevant
irresistible
irrevocable
irrigate
island

J

jeopardize
journey
judgment
junta

K

khaki
kibbutz
kilometer
kilowatt
knowledge

L

label
laissez faire
laser
league
legislature
leisure
leukemia
liable
liaison

libel
license
lieu
lieutenant
lightning
likable
likelihood
liquefy
liquor
logarithm

M

maintain
maintenance
malignant
maneuver
manila
margarine
marijuana
marital
marshal
martial
martyr
Massachusetts
massacre
mathematics
mediocre
megabyte
megawatt
memento
menstruation
metaphor
metastasize
microprocessor
migraine

mileage
milieu
miniature
minuscule
minutiae
miscellaneous
mischievous
missile
misspell
mnemonic
modem
monitor
mortgage
mustache

N

naive
necessary
neither
niece
noxious
nozzle
nuance
nuclear

O

occasion
occurrence
odyssey
ombudsman
omniscient
ophthalmologist
overrun

P

panacea
paradigm
parallel
parameter
paraphernalia
parliament
per diem
peremptory
perennial
peripheral
permissible
personnel
perspiration
pharmaceutical
phase (aspect)
    faze
Philippines
phosphorus
physician
placebo
plebiscite
pneumonia
poisonous
pollutant
polymer
porous
posthumous
precede
preferred
prerogative
prevalent
privilege
procedure
proceed

programmer
prophecy (noun)
prophesy (verb)
protein
protocol
pseudonym
publicly
Puerto Rico

Q

quasi
questionnaire
queue
quiche
quorum

R

rapport
rarefy
rebuttal
recede
receipt
receive
reciprocal
recommend
reconnaissance
recuperate
recurrence
referred
rehearsal
relevant
remittance
renaissance
renege

rescind
resistance
rhythm

S

saccharin (noun)
sacrilegious
satellite
scenario
schedule
scissors
secretary
seizure
separate
sergeant
siege
sight (vision)
    cite
    site
silhouette
similar
simulate
simultaneous
site (location)
    cite
    sight
skeptical
solar

sophomore
spaghetti
stratagem
strategy
stupefy
subpena
    (or subpoena)
subtle
succeed
superintendent
supersede
surprise
surveillance
syllable
synagogue
synonymous

T

tariff
thief
threshold
tobacco
tongue
toxin
trafficking
trauma
treasurer
trek

U

ubiquitous
unanimous
unnecessary
unprecedented
usage

V

vacuum
vehicle
vengeance
verbatim
veterinarian
vice versa
vicious
villain

W, Y, Z

waiver
weird
wholly
withheld
woolen
yield
zucchini

Index

Italicized words refer to the section entitled *Confused and Abused Words,* pp. 103-123.

Abbreviations, 12, 22, 44-47, 67
  capitalization of, 51
  comma following, 22
  plurals of, 12, 47, 60
Abstractions, 95-96
Acronyms, 10, 44-45, 60
  See Abbreviations
Active voice, 93-94, 128
Addresses, mailing, 45-46
Adjectives
  compound, 30, 131
  consecutive, 17-18
  defined, 85, 128, 135
  numeral-unit, 31
Adverbs
  conjunctive, 22
  defined, 85, 128, 136
Advice, Advise, 106
Affect, Effect, 106
Agreement
  of subject and pronoun,
    78-79
  of subject and verb, 70-78
Allude, Refer, 106
Allusion, Illusion, 106
Alright, 106
Alternate, Alternative, 107
Among, Between, 108
Ante, Anti, 107
Antecedent, 77, 128
Antonym, 128
Anxious, Eager, 107
Apostrophe, 6-12
  in abbreviations, 12
  in contractions, 11-12
  with possessives, 6-11
Appositive, 20, 129
Apt, Liable, Likely, 107

Articles
  defined, 129
  with acronyms, 45
As, Like, 117
Assure, Ensure, Insure, 116

Bad, Badly, 108
Beside, Besides, 108
Between, Among, 108
Bias, avoiding, 79, 101-102
Bi, Semi, 108
Bibliography, 140-142

Can, May, 109
Capital, Capitol, 109
Capitalization, 48-52
  of abbreviations, 51
  of captions, 52
  after colon, 12-13, 48
  of ethnic groups, 51
  of government agencies, 49-50
  of hyphenated words, 49
  of geographical terms, 50-51
  of seasons, 52
  of time of day, 52
  of titles, 48-49
Captions, 52
Case, 122, 129
Clauses
  coordinate, 14, 130
  defined, 130
  dependent, 15, 24, 100
  independent, 14-15, 17, 23, 24,
    38-39, 130-132
  nonrestrictive, 20, 120, 130
  restrictive, 20, 120, 130
  as subject, 72-73
Collective nouns, 74-75

Colon, 12-14
  capitalization following, 12-13,
    48
Comma, 14-24
  with appositives, 20, 129
  for clarity, 19
  with consecutive adjectives,
    17-18
  with conjunctive adverbs, 22
  for contrast, 19
  in direct address, 21
  in direct quotation, 22
  with independent clauses, 14-15
  with introductory phrases, 21
  with nonrestrictive elements, 20
  omission of words and, 19
  overuse of, 23-24
  with parenthetical phrases, 20
  for pauses, 19
  in series, 17, 24
Comma fault, 23, 39-40, 131
Complement, 86, 131
Complement, Compliment, 110
Complex sentence, 138
Compound, defined, 131
Compound predicate, 24
Compound sentence, 132, 138
Compound subject, 73-74, 132
Compound verb, 132
Compound words, 29-31, 59
  adjectives, 30-31, 131
  hyphenation of, 29-31
  improvised, 31
  nouns, 29
  numbers, 31, 49
  plurals of, 59-60
  possessives of, 10
Comprise, 110
Conjunctions
  coordinate, 14, 17, 132
  defined, 85, 132, 136
  joining independent clauses,
    14-15, 23
  subordinate, 132

Conjunctive adverbs, 22, 39
Contact, 110
Continual, Continuous, 110-111
Contractions, 8, 11-12, 67
Convince, Persuade, 111
Council, Counsel, Consul, 111

Dangling modifiers, 82-83, 132
Dash, 25-26
Dates, 23, 46
Dependent clauses, 15, 24, 100,
  130
Different from, Different than,
  111-112
Dilemma, 112
Direct object, 87, 135
Disburse, Disperse, 112
Discreet, Discrete, 112
Disinterested, Uninterested, 112
Disperse, Disburse, 112
Double Negative, 83-84, 133

Eager, Anxious, 107
Ecology, 112
Effect, Affect, 106
Either-or, 77-78
Ellipsis, 27
Em dash, 26
Emigrate, Immigrate, 112
Eminent, Imminent, 113
En dash, 26
Ensure, Insure, Assure, 116
Enthused, 113
Excess words, 90-93

Farther, Further, 113
Fewer, Less, 114
Figures, 55-56
Flammable, Inflammable, 114
Flaunt, Flout, 114
Footnotes, abbreviations in, 47
Foreign words
  italics with, 53
  plurals of, 61

Fractions, 31, 55, 78
Fulsome, 114
Further, Farther, 113

Geographic terms, 50-51
Get, Got, 114
Gerund, 133
Glossary, 128-139
Got, Get, 114
Grammar, 69-87
  agreement of subject and
    pronoun, 78-79
  agreement of subject and verb,
    70-78
  dangling modifiers, 82-83, 132
  double negatives, 83-84
  misplaced modifiers, 81-82, 134
  parallel construction, 80-81

Home, Hone, 115
Hopefully, 115
Hyphen, 28-32
  capitalization with, 49
  with compound numbers, 31
  with compound words, 29-31
  in fractions, 31
  in numeral-unit adjectives, 31
  with prefixes and suffixes, 28
  word division, 64-67

I, Me, Myself, 115
Idiom, 10, 30, 83, 133
Illusion, Allusion, 106
Immigrate, Emigrate, 112
Imminent, Eminent, 113
Imply, Infer, 116
Independent clauses, 14-15, 17,
  23, 39, 130
Indirect object, 87, 135
Infer, Imply, 116
Infinitive, 100, 133
Inflammable, Flammable, 114
Insure, Ensure, Assure, 116
Interjection, 134, 136

Irregardless, 116
Italics, 36, 53-54
It's, Its, 8, 116

Jargon, 98-100

Lay, Lie, 116
Lend, Loan, 117
Less, Fewer, 114
Liable, Likely, Apt, 107
Lie, Lay, 116
Like, As, 117
Likely, Liable, Apt, 107
Loan, Lend, 117
Loose, Lose, 117

May, Can, 109
Me, Myself, I, 115
Meantime, Meanwhile, 118
Measurement, units of, 56
Mechanics, 43-67
Misnomer, quotation marks
  with, 35
Misplaced Modifier, 81-82, 134
Misspelled words, 57-64, 143-148
Modifiers
  dangling, 82-83, 132
  misplaced, 81-82, 134
  punctuation with, 17-18, 24
  unit, 30, 131
Money, units of, 56, 78
Myself, I, Me, 115

Nauseated, Nauseous, 118
Negative, Double, 83-84, 133
Negative form, 95
Neither-nor, 77-78
Nominative case, 129
Nonrestrictive clauses, 20-21, 24,
  120, 130, 134
Nouns
  chains of, 99
  collective, 74-75
  compound, 29

Nouns *cont'd*
  defined, 84, 134, 135
  proper, 134
Number
  agreement of subject and verb,
    70-78
  agreement of subject and
    pronoun, 78-79
  defined, 70, 134
Numbers, 55-56
  compound, 31
  fractions, 31, 55, 78
  plurals of, 60
  spelling of, 55

Object, 87, 134-135
Objective case, 122-123, 129
Omission
  of letter or number, 11-12
  of word(s), 19, 27

Parallel construction, 80-81
Parentheses, 32-33
Participle, 135
Parts of speech, 84-87, 98,
  135-136
Passive voice, 93-94, 136
Person, 70-71, 87, 136
Persons, People, 118
Persuade, Convince, 111
Phrases
  with dashes, 25-26
  explanatory, 25, 39
  intervening, 72
  introductory, 21
  nonrestrictive, 20-21, 24, 120,
    130, 134
  parallel, 80-81
  parenthetical, 20, 25
  restrictive (defining), 20, 120,
    130, 138
  as subject, 72
Plurals
  of abbreviations, 12, 47

formation of, 58-61
possessive of, 7, 9
spelling of, 58-61
Positive form, 95
Possessive case
  with apostrophe, 6-10
  defined, 129, 136, 137
Predicate, 24, 86, 136
Predominant, Predominate, 119
Prefixes
  defined, 137
  hyphenation of, 28, 65
Preposition, 85, 136, 137
Principal, Principle, 119
Pronoun
  defined, 86, 135, 137
  indefinite, 75-76
  possessive, 8, 137
  relative, 77, 137
Proper names, 7, 134
Punctuation rules, 5-41
  apostrophe, 6-12
  colon, 12-14
  comma, 14-24
  dash, 25-26
  ellipsis, 27-28
  hyphen, 28-32
  parenthesis, 32-33
  quotation marks, 34-37
  semicolon, 38-40
  slash, 40-41

Quotation marks, 34-37
  direct quotation, 22, 34
  single quotation marks, 36
Quotations, italicizing, 54

Redundancies, 90-93
Refer, Allude, 106
Respectfully, Respectively, 119
Restrictive clauses, 20, 120, 130
Reverse Rules, 126-127

Salutations, 13, 23
Semi, Bi, 108
Semicolon, 15, 22, 38-39
  with independent clauses, 38
  in series, 38
Sentences
  complex, 138
  compound, 132, 138
  inverted order, 72
  length, 83-84, 100
Series, 16-17, 24, 28, 38
Shall, Will, 119
Spellcheckers, 57
Spelling, 57-64
Split infinitive, 133
Stanch, Staunch, 119
Stationary, Stationery, 119
Style, 89-102
Subject
  agreement of, 70-79
  defined, 86, 138
Subjective case, 129
Subordinate clauses,
  see Dependent Clauses
Suffixes
  addition of, 62-63
  defined, 139
  hyphenation of, 28, 65
Syllabication, 64-67
Synonym, 139

Tenant, Tenet, 120
That (adverbial), 120
That, Which, 120

That, Who, Whose, 121
Time, units of, 56, 78
Titles, 10, 14, 35, 46, 48-50, 53
Too, 121

Uninterested, Disinterested, 112
Unit modifier, 30, 55, 131

Vagueness, 95-96
Venolia's Reverse Rules, 126-127
Verbs
  agreement of subject and, 70-78
  compound, 132
  defined, 85, 136, 139
Very, use of the word, 101
Voice, 93-94, 128, 136

Was, Were, 122
Which, That, 120
Who, Whom, 122-123
Who, Whose, That, 121
Will, Shall, 119
Word division, 64-67
Words
  compound, possessive of, 10-11
  confused and abused, 103-123
  simple, 96
  trendy, 97
Would of, 123
Writing well, importance of, 2, 6,
  70, 90, 102

ZIP Code abbreviations, 45

OTHER BOOKS YOU MAY FIND USEFUL:

REWRITE RIGHT!
by Jan Venolia

How to review, edit, and rewrite any piece to make it clearer and more effective. Special section on non-sexist writing.

BETTER LETTERS
by Jan Venolia

An up-to-date handbook for improving your business and personal correspondence. Called "a treasury of literacy, full of good advice" by the Los Angeles Times.

WRITING AT WORK
by Ernst Jacobi

A style manual geared to those who must write for business purposes—covers everything from press releases to resumes, memos to reports.

QUOTE UNQUOTE
by Jonathan Williams

"Our most outlandish man of letters' answer to Bartlett's...it is unalloyedly delicious"—*Booklist*

A strange and wonderful collection of quotes from far and wide, from famous to obscure, from sublime to ridiculous.

PUBLISHER'S LUNCH
by Ernest Callenbach

A novel about how the publishing industry really works—must reading for all aspiring authors.

For more information, check your local bookstore or contact the publisher directly. Write for our free complete catalog of over 500 books and tapes.

TEN SPEED PRESS
P.O. Box 7123 • Berkeley, CA 94707 © 1-800-841-BOOK